Praise for *Surv...*

"Frank Thomas is not only one of our most dangerous preachers but also a teacher who hopes to instigate a new generation of dangerous preachers. If you know much of the preaching of Jesus Christ, you know why 'dangerous' is one of the highest compliments one can pay a preacher. Frank gives warm encouragement and practical guidance to embolden us preachers to preach Christ in risky, bold, life-giving ways."

—Will Willimon, professor of the practice of Christian ministry, Duke Divinity School, Duke University, Durham, NC; United Methodist bishop; author, *Who Lynched Willie Earle?, Fear of the Other*, and *Stories* from Abingdon Press

"Now more than ever, preachers are called to use words to heal. In this jewel of a book, Frank Thomas helps us do just that. *Surviving a Dangerous Sermon* shows us why truth-telling, empathy, and moral imagination are vital concerns for anyone who aspires to preach a word of hope. Thomas offers incisive and timely wisdom for 'such a time as this.'"

—Donyelle McCray, assistant professor of homiletics, Yale Divinity School, Yale University, New Haven, CT

"In the tradition of the civil rights movement, Frank Thomas encourages preachers to imagine a larger and more 'dangerous' moral vision that supersedes the worldviews of progressives, moderates, and conservatives. He then shows how an empathic understanding of persons holding these competing worldviews can help preachers survive after preaching such morally challenging sermons. Highly recommended."

—John S. McClure, Charles G. Finney Professor of Preaching and Worship, Vanderbilt Divinity School, Vanderbilt University, Nashville, TN

"Thomas calls the church to preach the gospel of a savior who subversively upended the hierarchical powers and nearly got thrown off of a cliff for doing so. The church is called to preach dangerous sermons that offer prophetic challenge. But to survive this sort of preaching, the gospel must be proclaimed with priestly empathy for the diversity of people to and for whom the gospel is preached. Thankfully, Thomas shows us how to walk the sermonic high wire with theological faithfulness, self-awareness, and contextual analysis."

—Lenny Luchetti, professor of proclamation and Christian ministry, Wesley Seminary, Indiana Wesleyan University, Marion, IN

"Frank Thomas's compelling sequel to *How to Preach a Dangerous Sermon* balms the wounded preacher's ruptured moral imagination and exposes the shortfalls of competing idolatries of 'working gospel' perspectives— perspectives that reinforce homiletical arrogance and exegetical myopia, and define America's pulpit polarization today. Seamlessly synthesizing homiletical theory, cognitive science, and practical wisdom, Thomas demonstrates why he is among the most prolific, creative, and respected scholar-teacher-practitioners in contemporary homiletics. *Surviving a Dangerous Sermon* is sage guidance for preaching an inclusive gospel before empathy-challenged, hope-vanquished Christians on the verge of vacating church pews never to return. This book inspires. It will change your preaching life for the better. After reading, you just might spend the balance of your lifetime trying to figure out how to justly return the favor."

—Kenyatta R. Gilbert, professor of homiletics, Howard University, Washington, DC; author, *Exodus Preaching: Crafting Sermons about Justice and Hope* from Abingdon Press

Other Abingdon Press Books
by Frank A. Thomas

How to Preach a Dangerous Sermon

Introduction to the Practice of African-American Preaching

American Dream 2.0

FRANK A. THOMAS

SURVIVING A
DANGEROUS
SERMON

Abingdon Press
Nashville

SURVIVING A DANGEROUS SERMON

Copyright© 2020 by Abingdon Press

Library of Congress Control Number: 2020932992

ISBN: 978-1-5018-9654-5

20 21 22 23 24 25 26 27 28 29—10 9 8 7 6 5 4 3 2 1
MANUFACTURED IN THE UNITED STATES OF AMERICA

To the Memory of
Reverend Doctor Charles Edward Booth
February 4, 1947–March 23, 2019

Prophetic preacher, mentor, teacher, author, friend, revivalist,
pastor, encourager of my gifts, stately and kind gentleman,
and friend of preachers everywhere.

Watch this prolific interview of Charles Edward Booth:
https://www.youtube.com/watch?v=kQaiNZXe96Y

To the Future of Our First Grandchild
August Elise Dickerson
Born May 4, 2018

Your grandparents believed and lived this:
We will not submit to any god, church, nation, president, party, flag, institution, narra-
tive, or economic or political system that demands we become a second-class citizen. We
will not abdicate our stature as created in the image of God, nor our right to be equal
based upon all of the sacrifice of our ancestors for this nation. Neither will we demand
consciously or unconsciously of any person that they be second class in regard to us. We
will be equal and respect everyone as equal. Before we will be a slave or slave master,
we will be buried in our grave and go home to our Lord and be free.

CONTENTS

vii

Contents

Contents

Contents

Foreword

Frank A. Thomas's spiritual DNA includes a vibrancy of interrogating and articulating faith claims in a world often void of nourishing spiritual fruit and consideration of human difference. He possesses the intellectual ability and verbal agility to at once mine and dispense profound homiletical methodologies and to challenge and persuade preachers and listeners to consider the spiritual costs and purposes of preaching. The "Word made flesh...," for Thomas, is to be spoken and understood as holy and wholly from God. It is not for human ownership, performance, and triviality, but for deepening one's connective tissue with God and God's promises and for undergirding our human response and responsibility to God.

Thomas states part of his rationale for *Surviving a Dangerous Sermon* is to be in conversation with preachers, laity, and those who might not regularly preach regarding processes and consequences of preaching about "unjust moral orders" and "moral hierarchies." Practitioners and professors of preaching, like Thomas, ground their engagement in the biblical text in their personal definition of preaching. I open homiletics classes asking each student to formulate and recite their personal understanding of the preaching event. These students are often laity, and they recite what their preaching mentor said, those who have minimal experience, or those who scoff at the necessity of preaching, particularly anything political or social.

After their responses, I offer my operating definition as one view of the discipline. The class then dissects these words:

The purpose of preaching is to present an acknowledged word of God concerning God's presence, power, passion, and purpose, regardless of translation verbally and nonverbally (vocally or nonvocally) with a particular listener (or gathering of listeners) who sense the impact of a perceived truth resulting in an impulse of change or conversion in his or her own life through the joy of possibilities and promise.

When one preaches, personal beliefs about who God is, how one names God, what attributes are ascribed to God, the depth of one's study of the texts, as well as relationality with listeners, one's social-political engagement, history, intelligence, and authenticity, character, and reputation are in plain sight. I propose one's faith, assessment of humanity, and prejudices are most vulnerable and exposed during the preaching moment.

I share that they are free to develop, expand, excise, or totally scrap my definition because I am clear this is my definition and there are millions of variations on the theme. We cover the reality their definition will change or be modified based on their individual denomination, sermonic experience, personal faith development, use of the biblical text, creative process, authority ascribed to the preacher, preaching models, feedback or critiques of sermons, education of the congregation and preacher, community, and culture or political sensibilities. Additionally, their semester-long small-group conversations discuss those "bad sermon days," those times when nothing falls into place, those times when the congregation is not responsive or rejects what is said, those times when the text says one thing but we preach something else out of fear of retaliation or manipulative or personal agenda, those times when despite our best efforts we miss the mark of the gospel, or those times when the preacher misreads the listeners, the context, or the event.

Frank A. Thomas presents an expansive methodology for *Surviving a Dangerous Sermon,* initially revisiting *How to Preach a Dangerous Sermon*. It is compelling he chose "surviving," originating in the intransitive and transitive verb *survive,* meaning to continue to function or prosper, to live on, to withstand, to last, or to remain alive after the cessation of something (Latin "superesse" or "supervīvere," equivalent to "super-," "super-" + "vīvere," to live). Having eloquently outlined how to preach a "dangerous" sermon in his previous book, Thomas now supplies his belief that the risk of sermonically engaging evil is not a death knell. He restates the necessity of meaningful, coherent, and lucid sermons regarding the unjust social political practices in the "religion of the American empire." He takes his time setting the stage for how to preach and survive to fight another day, initially by reminding the reader of his proposed theory and praxis in *How to Preach a Dangerous Sermon,* by close reiteration of his eclectic definition of the moral imagination through extensive theoretical evaluation of the "moral order of white supremacy" in the twenty-first century. Thomas's exploration of Andre Resner's "working gospel," Edward Farley's "bridge paradigm" as theological grounding, and George Lakoff's concepts of "dual moral orders and dominance hierarchies" provides a succinct yet critical undergirding for a preacher's comprehension of sermonic context.

My womanist passion for justice means seeking the humanity and survival/value of all persons. I have because of my physicality chosen to focus on those who look like me with particularity, but not exclusively. There are consequences to my choices. Yes, there are persons I have a difficult time loving. Yes, there are persons who hate my ability to breathe think, live, teach, preach, or love on my own. Yes, there are those who will never invite me to preach or teach in their "shop," "church," or "conference," but God did not give me a list of names or places that would prove I had arrived when I answered my call, so I am good. Thomas's insightful inclusion of both the "Strict Father" morality of conservative proclaimers and the "Nurturant Parent" morality of progressive proclaimers provides a stimulating and balanced evaluation of preacher worldviews, sermon content, sermon context, and how to navigate consequences of particular sermonic presentations. The third chapter assists in deeper understanding of the varieties of persons preaching and listening to sermons and raises awareness of the exigency of the preacher to remember context matters.

Long before I began teaching speech pathology and later homiletics, my parents taught me to think things through and consider the consequences before speaking. Their mantra was: "Say what you mean and mean what you say. Don't say it if you are not willing to stand behind your words. Remember, words hurt!" I encourage transformative preaching students to use textual integrity (this includes actually preaching the text cited), to investigate the facts on as many sides as possible, never to let their personal agenda blind them to the richness of the exegeted text, to know the purpose and occasion of the sermon, to check their own connection to—and complicity in—the subject matter being addressed, to avoid browbeating and denigrating, and to authentically seek substance over style. These are my homiletical (sermonic) values as a professor and as one who preaches often in a variety of settings, context, and audiences. One should always stand behind the words articulated when expounding on a biblical text. Everybody has a bad preaching day sometime. Everyone has had missteps. One who preaches has a responsibility to do no harm while sharing what God has instructed. Killing the sheep rather than pointing toward healing balm is not responsible sacred rhetoric.

Thomas follows his rhetorical examination with a deep probe into the events surrounding the "eulogy" for Aretha Franklin on August 30, 2018, which he terms a "dangerous sermon." He deconstructs the eulogy and analyzes select responses of laity, clergy, preaching professors, family, the eulogist, and media. He skillfully, in five movements, exegetes Rev. Dr. Jasper Williams Jr.'s sermon, the effect of the discussion on social media, the difference between a local pulpit and a worldwide stage, and how one handles critique. As one of the preaching professors who assessed the eulogy, I wrote:

> I know the pain and difficulty of planning and executing the funeral of a parent, spouse, sibling, and friend. That being said, eulogies always cause me pause. They are weighted with so much stuff and by definition are supposed to be a speech or piece of writing praising (honoring, lifting up, celebrating, recounting deeds, highly regarding) a person recently deceased. Regardless of the length of service or what precedes or follows the eulogy, the color of the flowers or casket, the number of dignitaries, the music or ignored timed remarks, the tears or laughs, the shouts or silence, the obituary or condolences, the age, name, reputation, or status of the chosen eulogist, or the eulogist's sociopolitical-theological beliefs, the speech/sermon/talk is supposed to be about the person who is being funeralized and to

leave a lasting, comforting memorial for the family, friends, and gathered congregation.

As my parents ingrained in me, I stand by my words. Dangerous sermons are ultimately about naming evil and proposing change. Dangerous sermons receive pushback. Dangerous sermons may also wound the guilty and the innocent. The presence of colliding worldviews, knowledge of one's working theology, the reality of varied social, spiritual, and political leanings, an abundance of strategies to address to critical "-isms," the choice of descriptive vocabulary, and the potential of critique by those holding differing moral ethical opinions are essential to surviving a dangerous sermon. Change hurts but is necessary. Verbally risking one's thoughts, beliefs, reputation, character, position, and, in extreme cases, one's life to address moral ethical issues is dangerous yet survivable.

In *Surviving a Dangerous Sermon*, Thomas proposes that we sermonically begin the work toward wholeness through pointing toward the danger, finding words to describe it, accepting our own complicity in death-dealing situations, inspiring others to live above the stuff of the world while seeking change, and remaining open to internal and external survival techniques.

My mother used to play a song that began, "In times like these we need a Savior..." We perpetually live in times that require a risking, regenerating, redeeming Word from the voices of faith God has assigned to remind us that God is still in control. Preachers are called to "tell a dying world Jesus lives." Called and anointed proclaimers recite those who "have put their hand on the plow and will not turn back." This book provides fresh preaching manna, study resources, and a community of preachers willing to accept the challenge of preaching and surviving dangerous sermons.

I am reminded, in true preaching manner, the prophet Isaiah described the call for justice proclaimers and practitioners in chapter sixty-one and stated in verse eight that God loves justice. Jesus reiterated the same theme in Luke 4:16-19. The world needs bold witnesses of God's emancipating power. Thomas, many liberation proclaimers, and I have a testimony that it will not be easy, but you are not alone. Most importantly as you preach,

that same God of justice, embodied in Jesus Christ and energized by the
Spirit, is with you.

Teresa Fry Brown, PhD
Bandy Professor of Preaching
Candler School of Theology, Emory University, Atlanta, Georgia

Executive Director of Research and Scholarship,
African Methodist Episcopal Church

WHAT REALLY IS A DANGEROUS SERMON?

The congregation often looks to religion not as an external force that places radical demands on their lives, but rather as a way to fulfill their needs. Those who are successful in the world, those of abundant means, those in positions of power (whether they are aware of this power or not), rarely come to church to have their social and economic powered altered.... Thus, if they can go to either the Church of Meaning and Belonging, or the Church of Sacrifice for Meaning and Belonging, most people will choose the former. It provides benefit for less cost.

—Michael O. Emerson and Christian Smith

After the 2018 publication of *How to Preach a Dangerous Sermon*, many have frequently asked essentially the very same questions after lectures, presentations, and conversations about the book: "What really is a dangerous sermon?" and "How do you survive (remain employed) after preaching dangerous sermons?"[1] Very plainly and simply, a dangerous sermon is a sermon based in the preacher's moral imagination that upends and challenges the dominant moral hierarchy that operates in the church and/or cultural context of the preaching event. When I offer this definition, it is necessary to quickly clarify that moral systems are not neutral and have embedded and often unexamined dominance hierarchies. George Lakoff, of whom I will say more later, clarifies the moral order of

---

1. Frank A. Thomas, *How to Preach a Dangerous Sermon* (Nashville: Abingdon Press, 2018).

dominance hierarchies: "Moral hierarchy projects dominance hierarchy onto the moral domain of legitimate moral authority, assuming that the most moral should rule. This is considered as just, and power *should* and by right rest with the most moral... the hierarchy limits the freedom of those lower on the hierarchy by legitimating the power of those higher on the hierarchy."[2] In its simplest form, dominance hierarchy is the reality that the most moral are at the top of the freedom, resource, and legitimacy food chain and the least moral are at the bottom. The people at the top are "winners" and have authority, assets, and legitimacy, while people at the bottom are deservedly "losers" with limited capacity to share in the resources of freedom, power, and wealth. Dominance hierarchy often functions to explain and justify position and rank in the moral order: people on top legitimize their rule, wherein people at the bottom based upon inferior talent or lifestyle choices are rightly obligated to follow.

A dangerous sermon challenges unjust moral orders and dominance hierarchies and the resulting misallocation of freedom, resources, assets, and legitimacy. A dangerous sermon disrupts the legitimacy of the oppressive moral order that operates smoothly, efficiently, and often silently in the economic, political, cultural, and religious structures of a given society. The bottom line of the dangerous sermon is the position and benefits of the "winners" at the top are challenged in light of the process of systemic delegitimizing and orchestration of the deserved "losers" at the bottom.

In response to the second question, how to preach dangerous sermons and survive, this book explores the reality that when we seek to preach dangerous sermons and challenge dominance hierarchies, we must think more deeply and broadly about the moral imagination of the audiences that we are addressing and challenging. In this age of the ubiquitous internet, far too many people throw around time-worn labels, stereotypes, talking points, dog-whistle phrases, prejudices, racist tropes, conspiracy theories, fake news, alternative facts, and scattered and unsubstantiated opinionizing ("some people are saying" or "many people are saying") most often heard on their favorite cable channel or internet sites. These sources

---

2. George Lakoff, *Moral Politics: How Liberals and Conservatives Think* (Chicago: University of Chicago Press, 2016), 431.

are trusted without discriminating and examining the accuracy of suppliers of the information presented. Based upon a "culture of outrage," very few people think carefully through their own moral values and the moral values of people on the "other side." Far too often, people on the other side are dismissed and portrayed as not having morals at all. In this regard, I am in complete agreement with T. S. Eliot who suggests:

> The number of people in possession of any criteria for discriminating between good and evil is very small . . . the number of the half-alive hungry for any form of spiritual experience, or for what offers itself as spiritual experience, high or low, good or bad is considerable. My own generation has not served them well. . . . Woe to the foolish prophets who have seen nothing.[3]

The number of people who have thought through deeply, profoundly, and carefully their moral values, and therefore are able to discriminate between good and evil is very small. In significant portions of the country, regardless of the facts, many people blindly follow the opinion of leaders. *Trump* For far too many people, their trusted leaders establish truth, that is, what is right and wrong and who is friend and enemy. Good is what my leader and group do and evil is what the other side does, regardless of the moral merits of behavior.

Moral order is a reality about which many laypeople have no understanding, and so they have not even considered it. The same can be said of preachers, many of whom have never thought deeply what moral order they subscribe to. This means that preachers have not sufficiently examined the moral order and the dominance hierarchies embedded in their theology and their preaching. Without close examination, some preachers have utilized their pulpits, knowingly or unknowingly, to justify and endorse the unjust moral order of American dominance hierarchy, which I deem to be preaching the religion of American empire. Many preachers attempt to be neutral and say nothing based upon potential negative consequences, and by their conspicuous silence they allow the status quo dominance hierarchy to continue aided and unchallenged. Therefore, my goal herein is twofold: (1) to help preachers preach sermons that assist

true!

---

3. T. S. Eliot, *After Strange Gods: A Primer of Modern Heresy* (London: Faber and Faber Limited, 1934), 61.

laypeople and congregations to more carefully discern their moral hierarchy and the moral hierarchy of others, especially those with which they might not agree, and (2) to help laypeople push, prod, encourage, and support preachers to preach in such a way that helps the congregation to be more discerning of their moral hierarchy and that of others.

The reality is that many religious leaders are up against very difficult odds preaching dangerous sermons. Many in the church see religion, as pointed out by Michael O. Emerson and Christian Smith in *Divided by Faith: Evangelical Religion and the Problem of Race in America,* "not as an external force that places radical demands on their lives, but rather as a way to fulfill their needs."[4] Even if clergy desire to work for social change, they are very often limited and circumscribed by their congregation. Unless the message is in the self-interest of their congregational group, most clergy end up softening the prophetic voice in favor of meeting "within-group needs."[5] Emerson and Smith quote Jeffrey Hadden, who studied clergy who participated in a one-month study at the Urban Training Center for Christian Mission (UTC) in Chicago in 1965. The program was attended by forty-eight Protestant clergy (all male and all white but one) and was designed to better equip them to minister in the inner city. In the city of Chicago, conflicts arose over educational policy and leadership in Chicago's public schools, centering on race. Civil rights leaders scheduled three days of marches from Soldiers Field to City Hall. Trainees were informed of the protest and encouraged to participate, and training was suspended to make it possible to do so. Hadden examined the UTC trainees and found that twenty-five of the forty-eight had been arrested.

Hadden examined why these twenty-five took more extreme actions leading to arrest. The question he sought to answer was, Were those who were arrested more committed to social justice for African Americans than those who were not arrested? Or were they more "constitutionally" inclined to being arrested? Hadden found no difference in these characteristics but found that the critical variable was the clergy members' "structural freedom." The four clergy who pastored integrated inner-city churches

4. Michael O. Emerson and Christian Smith, *Divided by Faith: Evangelical Religion and the Problem of Race in America* (New York: Oxford University Press, 2000), 164.

5. Emerson and Smith, *Divided by Faith,* 164.

and were supportive of the marches were arrested. Of the nine clergy who were not pastors, all but two—or 78 percent—were arrested. Of the clergy who pastored white city churches, only 37 percent were arrested. Of the ten clergy who pastored white suburban churches, just one was arrested. Four of the ten in this group not only failed to be arrested but also did not march in any of the demonstrations. Hadden concludes that the most significant factor in their decision whether or not to march was not their personal views or denominational position or the position of the UTC staff or the actions of their fellow ministers in the training program, but their congregation's expectation.

The clergy's prophetic voices were activated or constrained by their congregations based upon the congregation's felt needs:

> Clergy have come to see the church as an institution for challenging [people] to new hopes and new visions of a better world. Laity, on the other hand, are in large part committed to the view that the church should be a source of comfort for them in a troubled world. They are essentially consumers rather than producers of the church's love and concern for the world, and the large majority deeply resent [the clergy's] efforts to remake the church.[6]

This reality is the source and legitimization of the question asked of me all over this country: "How do I survive a dangerous sermon?"

In order to help preachers, my intent is to help them think carefully and deeply about their own moral imagination. I want preachers to preach effective and dangerous sermons that upend oppressive moral hierarchy. When a preacher thinks deeply about their own moral hierarchy and the moral hierarchies of the audience, the sermon can be crafted in such a way that it has the best chance to be heard, even when the congregation or parts of the congregation disagree with the preacher. Many preachers preach dangerous sermons, upending the moral order and hierarchy, and do not understand their own moral hierarchy and the moral hierarchy of the audience, both those that agree and disagree. This lack of under-standing of the preacher's and congregation's moral hierarchy is "an ac-cident waiting to happen," and the dangerous sermon can produce many

---

6. Emerson and Smith, *Divided by Faith*, 165–66.

casualties in which people and preachers are hurt and damaged and, worst of all, end up more entrenched in their position than before the sermon began. It is my hope that the careful preparation and understanding of moral hierarchy and theology that I propagate within this book give the preacher the best chance to help people grapple with the moral humanity of people with whom they disagree. Certainly, it does not always work out that there is this understanding. My aim is for the preacher to do the preparatory work—the moral and theological reflection—and to practice the rhetorical dexterity required to give the message the best chance to be heard by various audiences, and then to leave the work of change to God

Additionally, sometimes laypersons may be ahead of the preacher in having thought through their own moral imagination and those with whom they disagree. These laypersons can be a resource in helping the preacher and the congregation. Many times in my ministry, I have been pushed forward by the insight and clarity of an intellectually careful and spiritually loving layperson, who opened up new domains of thinking in my moral imagination and theology. I intend this book to be a resource for such laypersons. I am not interested in helping laypersons who seek to correct the minister, grind axes, set the minister straight, or any such negative and belittling behavior that seeks to limit the "structural freedom" of the minister. I am interested in assisting and equipping laypersons who want genuine dialogue and want the very best of unity and understanding for the minister and the congregation. I have grown immensely through relationships with such spiritually mature laypersons, and these persons need critical resources. My intent is that this book is an aid and a helpful resources.

Before further outlining the direction and content of the book, I want to briefly recap the concept of moral imagination and empathy and moral imagination and the church from *How to Preach a Dangerous Sermon*. The recap is necessary to move forward into deeper and more thoughtful analysis of moral hierarchy. I want to look briefly at the role of empathy and human imagination based in the thinking of philosopher David Hume.

Moral Imagination and Empathy

The best way to begin discerning moral imagination and dominance hierarchies is to wrestle with the issue of equality. Whom do I see as equal? Particularly, can I envision someone outside my group as equal? In my maleness, I have to search out as to whether or not I regard women as my equal. If I am a straight person, I have to discern if members of the LGBTQI community are really my equal. Are immigrants my equal? Are people from another race, ethnicity, or religious background my equal? And then a more difficult question is, Whom do the social structures, systems, and institutions of society treat as equal? For example, who is really equal before the law when minorities get different sentencing for the same crime as whites. The answer to these questions reveals a moral and dominance hierarchy. And whenever the preacher challenges and upends the oppressive moral hierarchy the sermon becomes dangerous.

David Hume argues that human beings are strongly governed by the imagination. Imagination is responsible for both the individual human mind and social arrangements that human beings form collectively. Hume believes that the imagination explains how we form "abstract" or "general" ideas; how we reason from causes to their effects, or from effects to their causes; why we tend to sympathize, or share the feelings of other people; why we project some of our feelings onto objects in the world around us; and the numerous "actions" that we believe. Concerning human social arrangements, he argues that the imagination explains why we form governments and shape the laws that we adopt, including those laws that govern the distribution of property and the passage of national authority from one leader to the next.

In Hume's view, to "sympathize" is to share the feelings of a person whom one encounters. Hume argues that moral sentiments—the approval that we feel when considering someone's virtues, and the disapproval when considering that person's vices—derive from sympathy. As people become more distant from each other in space and time, ideas of them and their passions become less strongly associated with our forceful and vivacious perceptions of ourselves; we therefore sympathize less strongly with them.

Dov Seidman, author, businessman, and generative moral thought-leader, applied Hume's insights about empathy to our contemporary American culture and argues that as distance increases between people, moral imagination decreases, hence less sympathy and more outrage.[7]

Seidman suggests that with cheap, ubiquitous, and easy-to-use tools of division, such as Twitter, undermining American unity is so common that it is difficult to even find a way to disagree respectfully, let alone accomplish unity. For Seidman, elections are contests of candidates, platforms, and visions, but the 2016 American presidential election was an election of protest. Sixty percent of the electorate wanted to disrupt, not just Washington, but also "the system," (i.e., capitalism, the economy— "the whole thing") because they believed "the system was rigged."[8] Compounding the problem was the rapid development of an "industry of anger" within many communication structures, where money is being made whipping up people into a frenzy of outrage. It was clear to him that America was being broken apart by communication tools of division and profits of the industry of outrage. It is clear from the Mueller report that even Russia and Russian operatives stoked division through the use of targeted and social media propaganda, influencing the presidential election in favor of Donald J. Trump. Americans were being divided by the global sabotage of a foreign government.

Seidman argues that we live in a "no distance" world, which leads quickly to moral arousal (outrage); and when we are outraged, we are more focused on "freedom from"—or casting off—disruption, rather than "freedom to." In this state of moral arousal, the tendency is to skip conversation and dialogue and to go straight to resolution: "fire the bums," "take the name off the building," or "lock her up." The opposite of moral arousal is moral progress, and where there is moral progress, there is nuance, equanimity, patience, deliberation, multiple conversations, and unwearied and unhurried dialogue.

7. "The Great American Divide with Hamza Yusuf," Davos World Economic Forum Annual Meeting 2017, YouTube, January 20, 2017, https://www.youtube.com/watch?v=uge3NuBHCuA; "Dov Seidman at the 2016 Fortune-Time Global Forum," Fortune + Time Global Forum Rome 2016 Fortune Magazine (December 2, 2016), https://www.youtube.com/watch?v=B2ZqEBLk1-8.

8. "The Great American Divide with Hamza Yusuf."

But in the culture of outrage, there is little time and space for the nuances of morality. The one who is outraged demands immediate relief. Some forms of oppression and violence warrant outrage and immediate relief, but it is wise to remember that ultimate truth is found in the domain of nuance and discussion. When we "throw the bums out," we get resolution but make no moral progress. Often, we will have no plan for the moral progress of community beyond our immediate outrage and disruption.

I want to suggest that we have lost much of the sense of empathy in this nation, and whenever empathy is lost, moral progress is hindered and shackled. The result is that we only have empathy for people of our group or tribe. In this environment, what is the role of the church?

The Church and Moral Imagination

According to Edmund Burke, the spirit of religion has long sustained moral imagination. This means that if moral imagination in America is limited, we must correspondingly conclude that there is a lack of moral imagination in the religion and contemporary church of America. If we believe T. S. Eliot, that the number of people in possession of any criteria to distinguish between good and evil is very small, and people are in search of what offers itself as spiritual experience, good or bad, then we must conclude that the church has not served the moral imagination of the people well. As Eliot said, "Woe to us as foolish prophets that follow our own spirit and have seen nothing." Eliot's statement suggests that foolish prophets follow their own spirit, make their own pronunciations, and have seen nothing from God. Eliot indicts the majority of the American Christian church. Based upon the lack of empathy in this country, I would argue that the church and its prophets have seen nothing. I once read this on a poster and I have never forgotten it: "You do not need religion to have morals. If you cannot determine right from wrong, then you lack empathy not religion."

My argument is that the church has participated in establishing a theological dominance hierarchy closely aligned to the dominance hierarchy in the culture, centered around establishing theological supremacy of one's own interpretation of the gospel as the only legitimate interpretation. Moral imagination is required to take up this challenge of an inclusive gospel, but far too much of the contemporary Christian church in the second decade of the twenty-first century has served as the handmaiden for the dominance hierarchy of the empire of America. In too many instances, the church has endorsed, propagated, supported, and given religious cover to the limited moral imagination of America. Let me now set forth the summary and imaginative flow of this book.

Imaginative Flow and Summary of *Surviving a Dangerous Sermon*

In theological circles, we overtly or covertly argue theological supremacy and legitimacy of our own gospel interpretation above all else and all others, and thereby we establish a theological dominance hierarchy that we mix with culture to support a cultural dominance hierarchy. In the attempt to foster more understanding between different theological circles and perspectives and examine cultural dominance hierarchy, in the first chapter, I will explore Andre Resner's concept of "working gospel," which leads us to explore Ed Farley's critique of the "bridge paradigm" of contemporary preaching. I will close the chapter with exploration of the question as to whether we preach the Bible or the gospel, and, in response to this question ask, What then is the relationship between the Bible and the gospel?

In the second chapter, I will explore the working gospel of the apostle Paul's "theology of the cross," return to further discussion of the bridge paradigm and the mystery of the gospel, and close the chapter by exploring my own working gospel that follows Luke's revelation and explanation of Jesus as the prophetic Messiah based in Luke 4:14-30. My sense was that after all this discussion of working gospel, it would be fair to the reader for me to expose my working gospel.

In the third chapter, I will intricately explore the work of the aforementioned distinguished professor of cognitive science and linguistics, George Lakoff, and his concept of dual moral orders and dominance hierarchies operating in America: (1) the Strict Father morality of conservatives and (2) the Nurturant Parent morality of progressives. The explanation and understanding of these moral paradigms will give the reader a foundation for understanding the worldviews of different moral communities.

My assertion is that it is helpful in surviving dangerous sermons if the preacher has an understanding of and can communicate with both moral orders, based upon the high likelihood that in most churches both moral orders are in the audience. And if both are not represented, it is important that people are helped to understand the moral order that is not present. This chapter attempts to give the preacher a certain moral and rhetorical agility to go well beyond glib religious and cultural usage of labels, stereotypes, tribal tropes, prejudices, divisive language, and especially demonization to speak to the heart of the faith tradition that brings people together by inspiring wonder, mystery, and hope rather than division and polarization.

In the fourth chapter, I will do a close reading of Rev. Jasper Williams Jr.'s dangerous sermon (eulogy) at the celebration of the life of Aretha Franklin, delivered on August 30, 2018. Aretha Franklin is a worldwide icon, and the funeral service attracted a global audience. Williams called a press conference to announce he was preaching the eulogy. After the eulogy, there was such passionate criticism and affirmation of his words in the African American community, that he held another press conference to discuss the eulogy.

I want to critically examine the eulogy, the press conferences, and the reaction to the eulogy in the black community, including the response of the Franklin family. I will utilize Lakoff's concept of dual moral orders and Resner's concept of working gospel to understand the dynamics around the speech. In the final analysis, my goal will be to look at Williams's persuasive strategies and to make suggestions as to how Williams and any preacher of dangerous sermons might reach as many people as possible, potentially even those of another moral order.

In the fifth chapter, I discuss practical strategies to survive a dangerous sermon. My intent is for this chapter to be very practical based upon my experience and observations with dangerous sermons across many years of preaching and studying preaching. I open the chapter connecting prophetic rhetoric with my concept of the dangerous sermon by exploring C. Cathleen Kaveny's discussion of prophetic discourse in the public square. Following Kaveny, I then list practical suggestions for surviving a dangerous sermon. These include such concerns as whether or not every sermon can or should be a dangerous sermon, the relationship between pastoral care of the people and a dangerous sermon, and so on. I offer several observations for consideration for the preacher who wants to survive a dangerous sermon. My suggestions are not guaranteed to work, but I assure the reader that they will help clarify their thinking on their own moral order and dominance hierarchy while the sermon is being prepared.

I close the chapter by presenting two of my own dangerous sermons as an example of all of the theory and methodology contained herein. The sermons represents the struggle for an inclusive gospel that builds bridges to connect people rather than preaching that continues to perpetuate division and polarizations. I also include study guide questions to help the reader reflect upon how they can preach dangerous sermons that attempt to reach dual moral orders.

Admittedly, the first three chapters of this book lay out a tremendous amount of theory, and the last two are more based in practical application. There are those who love theory and gravitate toward the explanation of theory as key to understanding. These readers prioritize theory first, and when they understand theory, then they are ready for practical application. And there are others who prefer practical application first and then relate to theory through the lens of application. These readers process from practical application to theory and then back to practical application. If you are of the former and access theory first, then please feel free to read the book in the normal manner of starting with chapter 1 and proceeding all the way to the closing sermons. If you value practical application first, then you can start with chapters 4 and 5 and then work your way back to chapters 1, 2, and 3. There is no right or wrong method of reading. Based upon your interest and learning style, start where you would like and with what works for you. The way that you process this book and its thesis is completely up to you and your moral imagination.

It is my view that preachers who want to survive a dangerous sermon should examine their own working gospel, their moral worldview and order, and the dominance hierarchies embedded therein. They must examine the audience's moral worldview and order, and the audience's dominance hierarchy. This process empowers the preacher to shape a sermon that has the best chance to be heard by the broadest number of people possible. Over time, the preacher who is attuned to different moral orders and working gospels will acquire a moral dexterity. This preacher will have the ability to develop messages that invite people, messages that go beyond common accidental and unintentional divisive rhetoric and polarizations, and messages that speak to the heart of the inclusive faith tradition, bringing people together by inspiring wonder, mystery, and hope.

I want to thank my wife, Joyce Scott Thomas, for the unwavering support and space to write and develop this manuscript. She knows that her husband would not stay sane if he could not write to express thoughts, reflections, and feelings. I am deeply appreciative of Christian Theological Seminary for allowing a research leave to work out my reflections despite my leadership of a busy and growing PhD program in African American Preaching and Sacred Rhetoric. Thanks to the PhD team for carrying on in my absence in such a marvelous way that allowed me to be minimally interrupted. I am grateful to President David M. Mellott, Dean Leah Gunning-Francis, Aimee Laramore, Kimberly D. Russaw, Courtney Buggs, and the entire faculty. I am appreciative of McCormick Theological Seminary for allowing space for a "writing retreat" to get this manuscript completed. My editor, Connie Stella, is a brilliant and constant encourager who allows my imagination and ideas to flow without censure. Thank you! We are at three books together and counting. Thanks to all of my students, teachers, colleagues, mentors, and friends. I am blessed that my parents, John Frank Thomas and Almetha King Thomas, are still alive to read and bless my writing and work. Thank you to my daughter, Rachel Dickerson, and son-in-law, Milton, for the support and blessing of August Elise Dickerson, our first grandchild. Many thanks to my sister Angela Edwards for the support and encouragement. Quoting Valerie Bridgeman, we are "stupid-in-love." Finally, to all the students that I have taught, in all the places and levels that I have taught, from PhD to no degree at all, you have helped me to clarify my thoughts and sharpen my ideas. Thank you.

My prayer is that God would grant us courage and grace to preach dangerous sermons that reach as many people as possible.

Frank A. Thomas
March 1, 2020

Chapter One

THE WORKING GOSPEL AND THE BRIDGE PARADIGM

The preacher is a theologian of the Word. She or he stands up in front of God and everybody and wrestles with what the scriptures say in all their diversity (for one, because the scriptures themselves embody various theologies and do not agree). There is no way of doing so apart from a careful act of theological reflection on the gospel. This is what makes preachers residential theologians of the gospel wherever they are.

—David Jacobsen

I graduated from Chicago Theological Seminary on the south side of Chicago in 1981. The scriptural text of Luke 4:18-19 was hammered into my head and heart as the sum total of Jesus's prophetic call and ministry, and therefore, in following Jesus, the synopsis of my ministry and developing call. This was the text that I heard over and over again in class, readings, teachings, peer discussions, sermons, and lectures:

> The Spirit of the Lord is upon me, because the Lord has anointed me.
> He has sent me to preach good news to the poor,
> > to proclaim release to the prisoners,
> > and to proclaim the year of the Lord's favor. (Luke 4:18-19)

We were trained for social justice ministry and delivering prophetic word/ action to people, churches, communities, religious institutions, economic systems, and political structures.

We also were warned that prophetic ministry was hard and not very popular. Growing up in segregated Chicago, I had sufficient experience and anger at injustice and racism in order to form my own bias toward prophetic ministry. I expected that just as Jesus's prophetic words in this Lukan text led to the hometown folks attempting to throw him off the cliff, I would be treated likewise. I was young, overzealous, with a strong measure of righteous indignation, and, as I once heard Fred B. Craddock say, "knew everything and knew nothing." Notwithstanding the mistakes of my early zeal, across my forty years of ministry, this Lukan text is the heart and crux of my "working gospel," and I have diligently labored not to assume that my working gospel is the only legitimate gospel.

In fact, far too many of us in theological circles spend far too much time establishing theological supremacy by arguing that our working gospel is the only legitimate gospel. For example, on September 4, 2018, "The Statement on Social Justice and the Gospel" was released with prominent Bible teacher John MacArthur as the founding signatory.[1] In the introduction, the Statement reads:

> Specifically, we are deeply concerned that values borrowed from secular culture are currently undermining Scripture in the areas of race and ethnicity, manhood and womanhood, and human sexuality. The Bible's teaching on each of these subjects is being challenged under the broad and somewhat nebulous rubric of concern for "social justice." If the doctrines of God's Word are not uncompromisingly reasserted and defended at these points, there is every reason to anticipate that these dangerous ideas and corrupted moral values will spread their influence into other realms of biblical doctrines and principles.

The Statement goes on at another point to say:

> And we emphatically deny that lectures on social issues (or activism aimed at reshaping wider culture) are as vital to the life and health of the church

---

1. "The Statement on Social Justice and the Gospel," https://statementonsocialjustice.com, John McArthur, Founding Signatory, September 4, 2018.

as the preaching of the gospel and the exposition of Scripture. Historically, such things tend to become distractions that inevitably lead to departures from the gospel.

At its base, this statement dismisses the experience of millions of Christians working for social justice, and is a form theological arrogance that supports the cultural dominance hierarchy of white supremacy. This statement emphatically states that marginalized people do not have the right to meet and interpret the God of scripture from their oppressed social location and believe that God is actively involved in their quest for spiritual and political freedom.

As a result of the damage of these kinds of divisive statements of dominance, my goal is to help preachers become honest about the fact that all preachers have a "working gospel" and, if they are not careful, their working gospel becomes embedded in their cultural and religious dominance hierarchy. When we present our working gospel as "the gospel" and thereby seek to make our interpretation normative for all people, we make our working gospel part of our dominance hierarchy. We operate out of a pseudo-legitimacy as definers of the authoritative interpretation of the text, and ignore the fact that there is such a thing as heresy. From the perspective of marginalized people, heresy is a working gospel that serves to justify privilege, racism, institutional discrimination, conquest, seizing of land, extermination and enslaving of people, the theft of resources of empire, and the like. A tremendous amount of conflict and violence is caused by a belief in the superiority of one's own gospel as the complete and conclusive gospel.

The reality is that many working gospels have always been and are still being preached today that preachers de facto argue are grounded in the biblical text. In my research, a question was submitted to an online site: "Did Paul and the apostles preach the same gospel? If not, then how many gospels are there all together and what is the difference?" There is quite a bit of scholarly debate on the differences of the gospel of Paul and the gospel of Peter. The question as to how many gospels there are all together is more complex, but what is certain is, there are many working gospels. The discovery of the gnostic working gospels among the Nag

Hammadi documents uncovered in Egypt in the 1940s ignited a firestorm in theological circles over which are the legitimate gospels. Then we have the Apocrypha, a set of secret gospel texts included in the Latin Vulgate and Septuagint, but not in the Hebrew Bible. Catholic tradition considers these texts to be deuterocanonical. Protestants consider them apocryphal. History reveals the reality of many working gospels. I believe the sixty-six books of the Protestant Bible are the authoritative, divinely inspired word of God *and* the reality of a multiplicity of working gospels.

It would make the world a more just and safer place if we would own up to our working gospel and learn to respect the working gospel of others, so long as the working gospels does not justify dominance and oppression. As an alternative to delegitimizing the gospel of others, I will explore in detail the concept of "working gospel" as espoused by professor of homiletics André Resner.[2] For purposes of an overall illustration of working gospel, I would like to begin by offering a brief summary of several of the contemporary working gospels.

Contemporary Working Gospels in the American Context

I would like to briefly consider a few working gospels in the contemporary American context. This is not an exhaustive list, but a tangible starting point for us to practically reflect on the concept of working gospel. Some of the most prominent working gospels functioning in the American environment today would include: the gospel of American sentimentalism, the gospel of American exceptionalism, the prosperity gospel, the gospel of denominationalism, the evangelical gospel, and the social justice gospel.

---

2. André Resner, "Reading the Bible for Preaching the Gospel," in *Collected Papers of the 2008 Annual Meeting of the Academy of Homiletics,* paper presented at the annual meeting of The Academy of Homiletics, Boston, MA (December 7, 2008), 223; "Do You See This Woman? A Little Exercise in Homiletical Theology," in *Theologies of the Gospel in Context: The Crux of Homiletical Theology,* ed. David Schnasa Jacobsen (Eugene, OR: Cascade, 2017), 19–24; *Living In-Between: Lament, Justice, and the Persistence of the Gospel* (Eugene, OR: Wipf and Stock, 2015).

First, the gospel of American sentimentalism is the working gospel of American civil religion that especially manifests itself in times of national crisis and tragedy. For example, when a national day of mourning is declared, the cultural religion of America is often evoked through the great hymn of "Amazing Grace." As an example, former president Barack Obama sang "Amazing Grace" at the funeral of South Carolina senator Clementa Pinckney.[3] "Amazing Grace" played on bagpipes is a tradition at public funerals of civic and national heroes.

The hymn "Amazing Grace" is very loosely connected with two biblical texts. The hymn borrows "I once was lost but now am found. Was blind, but now, I see," from Luke 15:32 and John 9:25.[4] This working gospel has little to do with whether or not one is a Christian, but the habits of American citizenship and mourning in the face of a national tragedy. This is the sentimental gospel of American civil religion.

Second, the gospel of American exceptionalism is the belief in America as "the errand in the wilderness" and the vision of "a city set up on a hill," a paraphrase of Matthew 5:14 spoken by John Winthrop to his fellow passengers in 1619 in a sermon at sea on the *Arabella*, reminding them that New England was a model for future settlements and the "eyes of all the people are upon us."[5] According to Winthrop and Puritan ideology, America had a divine mission and their pilgrimage to America fulfilled biblical prophetic, apocalyptic, and eschatological visions. The "discovery" of America was a great revelatory and prophetic event in the course of progress of the church upon the earth in which God's divine providence transformed the locus of the history of redemption and salvation from the corrupted Old World to the New World. God had miraculously kept the American continent from discovery such that a new chosen people of true Christians could be a light to the world and convert First Americans to

---

3. Sarah L. Kaufman, "Why Obama's Singing of 'Amazing Grace' Is So Powerful," *Washington Post*, June 26, 2015, https://www.washingtonpost.com/news/arts-and-entertainment/wp/2015/06/26/why-obamas-singing-of-amazing-grace-is-so-powerful/?utm_term=.6662a0e9cc6d.

4. The lyrics to "Amazing Grace" can be found at http://www.gospelsonglyrics.net/a/amazing-grace.htm. Luke 15:32 (NIV) reads, "This brother of yours was dead and is alive again; he was lost and is found"; and John 9:25 (ASV) reads, "Whereas I was blind, now I see."

5. Satayagraha, "America's Covenant with God: John Winthtrop's 'City on a Hill' Speech (1630)," https://satyagraha.wordpress.com/2013/04/18/john-winthrops-city-on-a-hill-speech-1630/.

Christianity. This gospel centers around the theme that God has ordained the history and mission of America and has given it a superiority over other nations. American exceptionalism clothes America in a divine and scriptural mission as the best and brightest hope of humankind. Many preachers today still continue to mix, intermingle, and coalesce the Bible and the American flag and capitalist culture and preach a gospel of American exceptionalism.

Third, the peculiarly American gospel of prosperity—or sometimes called the health and wealth gospel, the gospel of success, or seed faith gospel—is the working gospel that provides an unequivocal message of health, wealth, and success to adherents. Sickness and poverty are curses that are to be broken by faith. Prosperity preaching often downplays social critique and focuses instead on an empowering, individualistic strategy of success and the acquisition of material possessions. Prosperity theology views the Bible as a contract between God and humans: if humans have faith in God, God will deliver security and prosperity. Displays of success and material blessing are signs of God's favor and blessing based in adherence to divine principles, such as faith, sowing seeds, positive speech, and visualization of miracles. Financial blessing, positive relationship, and physical well-being are always the will of God for the believer in the preaching of prosperity gospel.

Fourth, there is the working gospel of denominational affiliation. Many denominations are founded out of some individual's working gospel, and the tenets and beliefs of this working gospel become normative for faith adherents. Typically, the works, writings, and sermons of the founder are codified for study, analysis, interpretation, and dissemination. Often, much interpretation is grounded in the historical theological beliefs of the founder, whether it be Richard Allen and the African Methodist Episcopal Church, John Wesley and the Methodist church, Martin Luther and the Lutheran church, John Calvin and Calvinism, William Seymour and Pentecostalism, and on and on. Within the Catholic church, the working gospel and the interpretation flow from the top, such as the teachings and writings of the Pope, and strict adherence to the Pope's working gospel and interpretation is required. This is especially when the Pope speaks "ex cathedra" (infallible from "the chair") on doctrine and matters of faith or morals and addresses it to the entire world in his capacity as the universal shepherd of the Catholic church.

I remember my complete shock at denominational gospel when several members left a church of which I was a member because in our church we baptized in the name of the "Father, Son, and Holy Ghost" (the Trinity). They argued that, according to the scriptures, our baptism was not a legitimate baptism. They went to the "Jesus only" movement, where the only true baptism was to be baptized in Jesus's name. There was quite a vigorous theological debate with competing scriptures, and at a very early age, I saw how divisive denominational gospel could be. Such theological debates are commonplace in many denominations and are evidence of different working gospels.

Fifth is the working gospel of evangelicals. There is much discussion, claiming, reclaiming, denying, and re-branding of the term *evangelical*, given that 80 percent of evangelicals supported the candidacy of Donald J. Trump. In order to quickly define evangelicals, I want to use a tool that identified evangelical beliefs by respondents strongly agreeing to four statements:

1. The Bible is the highest authority for what I believe.
2. It is very important for me personally to encourage non-Christians to trust Jesus Christ as their Savior.
3. Jesus Christ's death on the cross is the only sacrifice that could remove the penalty of my sin.
4. Only those who trust in Jesus Christ alone as their Savior receive God's free gift of eternal salvation.[6]

The working gospel of evangelicalism is a major religious, economic, and political force in America, evidenced primarily in support for the Republican party by the Christian right.

Finally, the working gospel of social justice is a large working gospel movement in our time. Historically, the social justice gospel was a movement in North American Protestantism that applied Christian ethics to social

---

6. This tool was used by the National Association of Evangelicals and LifeWay research to identify evangelical beliefs. See "What Is an Evangelical?" National Association of Evangelicals (NAE), https://www.nae.net/what-is-an-evangelical/.

concerns, such as economic inequality, poverty, alcoholism, crime, racism, slums, an unclean environment, child labor, inadequate treatment of laborers, poor schools, and the danger of war. The work of the gospel is to help change and transform the social and economic conditions of people as well as the salvation of their souls. The term *social justice* was renewed on a mass scale in the work of the civil rights movement led by Martin Luther King Jr. and supported by many who wanted to see justice and equality for all American citizens. Contemporary social justice issues might include mass incarceration, sex trafficking, environmental justice, gender equality, equal rights for LGTBQI communities, police violence, and crony capitalism.

Many social gospel adherents could be identified under the umbrella of identity politics. Identity politics is the working gospel of taking seriously one's ethnicity, gender, race, or social location as an interpretive lens through which to view the biblical text and hence construction of theology. For me, the term *identity politics* does not have a negative connotation. It is popular to decry identity politics as the purview of minorities, referring to nonwhite people motivated by an irrational herd instinct to take political and religious positions based upon the interests and perspectives of social groups with which they identify. In fact, white people have utilized identity politics since their arrival upon American soil. Conquest, slavery, segregation, and so on were all based in identity politics. Identity politics in theology has existed since the beginning of interpretation, and for centuries, the identity politics of Europeans and Euro-Americans was considered the norm and standard by which theological inquiry could be shaped. In the late 1960s, James Cone inaugurated black theology in theological circles and, as a result, a new era of inclusive working gospel, in which the identity politics of women, Koreans, LatinX, LGBTQI, Womanists, the differently able, and their working gospels came to be of value and weight in homiletical and theological considerations.

I chose some of the most popular working gospels. Popular religion and piety, and all working gospels for that matter, in all of our collective finitude, must assert that we do not know it all and that the mystery of the infinite cannot be fully named. I will say more about popular piety, and the finitizing of the gospel in the next chapter. For now, I want to turn to preachers and their working gospels.

Preachers and Their Working Gospels

Every preacher has a constellation of culture, a family of origin, and ecclesiastical systems that influence, raise, and develop us from the earliest stages of life. Such systems include categories of gender, ethnicity, social and economic locations of neighborhood and class, as well as conditions of physical and mental health. Most preachers are heavily influenced by these systems as they shape both their theology and the sermon that flows out of that theology. In an article entitled "Do You See This Woman? A Little Exercise in Homiletical Theology," André Resner clarifies that every preacher has an in-process "synopsis of the faith, an encapsulation of the whole point of Christianity, Christian community, of what difference God makes in and for the world."[7] Resner labels this "a working understanding of the gospel": "the preacher's 'working understanding of the gospel' is the imaginative theological and hermeneutical force that drives the way the preacher conceives, plots, and delivers sermons, structures worship services in which those sermons live, move, and have their being."[8] Though we do not have time to explore it, David Jacobsen has tremendous synergy with Resner and agrees with the fact that preachers have different working understandings of the gospel:

> In practice, preaching requires preachers to have a *habitus,* some theological core wisdom about gospel that helps them to do their task.... Preachers fret rightly about getting from the text to sermon, but underlying this concern is their commission to go preach the *gospel.* In doing so, I start the process of theological worth with a provisional confession of the gospel, i.e. what I call confessional homiletical theology. Confessional homiletical theologians think about preaching as a theological enterprise beginning provisionally with gospel and brought into critical dialogue with texts, contexts, and situations. André Resner has given this provisional confessional move a name: "working gospel."[9]

---

7. Resner, "Do You See This Woman?" 17.

8. Resner, "Do You See This Woman?" 18.

9. See David Schnasa Jacobsen, "The Practice of Homiletical Theology in a Confessional Mode: An Interim Report on the Homiletical Theology Project," North American Academy of Homiletics meeting in Dallas, Texas (December 9, 2017), http://www.bu.edu/homiletical-theology-project," 31–32.

Not only based upon Resner and Jacobsen, but even with a cursory pe-
rusal of historical and contemporary theological debates, it is clear that
preachers can read the same Bible and texts yet witness to different working gospels. In essence, my main point is that many of us use the term
gospel, but in reality we are not talking about the same thing. When we use
the term *gospel*, most of us are referring to our working gospel. It is helpful
in an environment of meaningful dialogue among Christian adherents if
preachers would define what they mean gospel by clarifying their working gospel. For example, most would agree with Romans 1:16 (NRSV)
where Paul says, "For I am not ashamed of the gospel; it is the power of
God for salvation to everyone who has faith…" What each of us means,
consciously or unconsciously, when we affirm this text is that we are not
ashamed of our working gospel. Yet, we carry on in dialogue as if we are
using a common term and referring to the same thing. When I read John
MacArthur's "Statement on Social Justice and the Gospel," my overarching response was that we were not talking about the same gospel. He was
simply expressing his working gospel.

This complexity then raises a monumental question begging for clarification in the theology of every preacher: What is the relationship between
the Bible and the gospel? How does the Bible function in the preaching
of the gospel? Or, how does the bridge paradigm work in our working
gospel? Let's look closely at preaching the Bible and preaching the gospel.

The Bridge Paradigm

Resner identifies reflections by professor of homiletics Ed Farley as
the initial catalyst for his thinking about the concept of working gospel.[10]
Farley challenges the prevailing paradigm of preaching that uncritically
assumes that every passage from scripture, whether by means of the
lectionary or preacher's choice, contains a preachable "X" that results in a

---

10. See Edward Farley, "Preaching the Bible and Preaching the Gospel," *Theology Today,* 51, no. 1
(April 1994): 90–103, also in *Practicing Gospel: Unconventional Thoughts on the Practice of Ministry* (Louisville: John Knox, 2003), 71–82. Two other articles on prevailing assumptions about the relationship
of the Bible to preaching are conveniently gathered in *Practicing Gospel* as well: "Toward a New Paradigm of
Preaching" (pp. 83–92) and "Sacred Rhetoric: A Practical Theology of Preaching" (pp. 93–103).

preaching "theme" or "claim." Farley argues that the preacher who seeks the preachable truth of God in a delineated passage of the Bible faces an impossible task. The impossible task is that, for several reasons (stated in the footnote below), there may be nothing preachable in the text and the preacher that must find a way from the text to the sermon—that is, the preacher must invent the "X," the preachable element.[11] The preacher determines the preachable "X" of the text that is to be preached, such as a word, phrase, image, action, or the text as narrative. This preachable "X" is then made into a lesson for life and preached. On strict exegetical grounds, passages are not developed for lessons for life, and therefore the preacher must wring the preachable "X" out of the exegeted passage. The result is that the passage is not so much preached as it becomes something that provides the jumping-off point for the sermon. To discover the lesson for life, the preacher must abandon exegesis and move to "interpretation"—that is, to apply the preachable "X" to the life situation of the congregation. I will make a clarifying demonstration of Farley's thinking in the later section titled "Your Haters Are Your Elevators."

Altering a phrase from the Vietnam War, Farley says the preacher must kill the passage in order to preach on it:

> Thus the preacher is not really starting with the text but with the lesson for life she knows is pertinent to the congregation. Rhetorically, the sermon may sound like it marches from the passage to the situation. Actually, the route is the reverse, from the situation, the in-the-light-of problem, to a constructed X of the text. The passage or its preachable X is not really that-which-is-reached, but the rhetorical occasion that jump-starts the sermon. Interpreting the passage is a modification of the exegeted content so that the passage's lesson for life can be applied.[12]

caution: don't have the sermon planned before reading the scriptur[e]

The construction of the preachable "X" is what Farley calls "the bridge paradigm," and its failure is built in from the beginning, by virtue of its

---

11. For Farley those reasons would include (a) the passage is a delimited piece in a larger writing, (b) there is no guaranteed inerrancy about the writing at any level, (c) there may be no X (preachable truth) in the passage, (d) the content of the passage would be something that must be preached against, and (e) the passage may have a moralizable content, something that lends itself to a lesson for life rather than the gospel. See Farley, "Preaching the Bible and Preaching the Gospel," 96.

12. Farley, "Preaching the Bible and Preaching the Gospel," 97.

abandonment of the text. The preacher's task is to build a bridge from that which is preached (the truth of the specific passage) to the situation of the congregation.[13] The construction of the bridge is not necessarily based in exegesis. That which is preached is not the content of the passage of scripture or the gospel but the preacher's preachable "X." Farley argues that if we are not careful, we will preach passages of the Bible and not the gospel.

As distinct from the paradigm of the early church, for us in this contemporary moment, preaching is a weekly liturgical event. Jesus and the early church preachers were itinerant preachers proclaiming the impending reign of God and were not the preachers of scheduled weekly liturgical services. Farley says, "primitive Christian preaching as we find it on the pages of the New Testament was an itinerant tradition proclaiming the good news of salvation in Jesus Christ. It is somewhat anachronistic to compare what we now call preaching with the *kerisso* of Paul and other evangelists."[14] The fact that preaching is a weekly liturgical event can be a strong catalyst to preach the content of the passage as a weekly life lesson for hearers rather than as a gospel event through which we are saved.

Farley even questions the dissection of the Bible into chapter headings and verses as interpretation that helps to move the preacher from the big picture of the gospel to looking in these weekly divisions for a small lesson for life. The preacher looks at a partitioned text and then seeks to find a weekly lesson for living life, often disregarding the meaning of the whole message. Farley suggests this division and portioning is problematic:

> It is clear that to divide the Bible into necessarily true passages is only one way among many ways of thinking about the Bible, of being "biblical," of placing oneself under the power and influence of Scripture. Surely we can be moved and influenced by the *Iliad*, *King Lear*, or *The Color Purple* without dividing these great works into pericopes and assuming a necessary truth to each one. Why must this be done to Jeremiah or Paul?[15]

13. Farley, "Preaching the Bible and Preaching the Gospel," 93.

14. Farley, "Preaching the Bible and Preaching the Gospel," 93.

15. Farley, "Preaching the Bible and Preaching the Gospel," 95.

This atomistic approach to scripture and thinking of scripture as a collection of small units and segments helps the passage to become a jumping-off place for the sermon, and the gospel can be easily abandoned. Again, to discover the lesson for life, the preacher abandons exegesis and moves to "interpretation" in order to cross the bridge from passage to people.

Farley's argument is important because it leads to the struggle to clarify what one means by preaching the "gospel" as opposed to life lessons from the text. One could conclude that life lessons is the preaching of the gospel, but though Farley finds that problematic, one has clarified one's working gospel inclusive of distinct parts of the Bible and exclusive of others. As stated earlier, Christian preachers all use the term *gospel* but do not all mean the same thing. Resner identifies an often umentioned truth existing in the field of homiletics:

> One of the dirty little secrets about homiletics, the discipline that studies, writes about, and teaches preaching—that there is no consensus on what preachers and homileticians mean by the word *gospel*, and there is very little discussion about how a preacher's construal of gospel functions hermeneutically as the preacher engages the Bible with a view to its use in preaching.[16]

David Jacobsen, whom we quoted earlier, responds to both Farley and Resner and takes up the challenge of defining how the Bible functions in preaching. Jacobsen and others define the function of the Homiletical Theology Project as: "to place the theological task more squarely in the middle of the practice of preaching and in the field of homiletics."[17] Defining the relationship between the Bible and the gospel is a theological task that all preachers must engage in on at least a weekly basis. Jacobsen reminds us that all preachers are "residential theologians of the gospel wherever they are" and "all sermon preparation is actually theology."[18]

As promised, let me give a brief example to hopefully make Farley's bridge paradigm clear by discussion of a popular sermonic form or trope: "your haters are your elevators."

16. Resner, "Do You See This Woman?" 20.

17. Jacobsen, "The Practice of Homiletical Theology in a Confessional Mode," 31.

18. Jacobsen, "The Practice of Homiletical Theology in a Confessional Mode," 35.

Your Haters Are Your Elevators

First, let's look closely at the text in 1 Corinthians 1:18-25 (NRSV) for an example of how we find the preachable "X":

> For the message about the cross is foolishness to those who are perishing, but to us who are being saved it is the power of God. . . . Has not God made foolish the wisdom of the world? For since, in the wisdom of God, the world did not know God through wisdom, God decided, through the foolishness of our proclamation, to save those who believe. For Jews demand signs and Greeks desire wisdom, but we proclaim Christ crucified, a stumbling block to Jews and foolishness to Gentiles, but to those who are the called, both Jews and Greeks, Christ the power of God and the wisdom of God. For God's foolishness is wiser than human wisdom, and God's weakness is stronger than human strength.

Exegesis on this text suggests that the proclamation of a crucified man as the Lord of glory was a stumbling block to Jews and Gentiles. Paul's preaching was considered pure foolishness, and he and other proclaimers were treated as stupid, ridiculous, and absurd. Exegesis helps us catch the flavor of the absolute outrage and indignation at the proclamation of the Lord of glory as a crucified criminal. It would be similar to a person in our time, condemned to death in the electric chair for a capital crime, and a small band of believers claiming that the deceased was raised and is the Lord of glory. Paul said Jews were looking for a sign and Greeks were looking for wisdom, but a crucified savior was offensive and a stumbling block. In the reality of the Greco-Roman culture to which Paul preached, a crucified Lord of glory was scandalous, embarrassing, humiliating, and shameful.

The preacher looking for the preachable "X" will transition from this exegesis to the interpretation of a life lesson from the text. One lesson would be to focus on "haters" in the contemporary context. Haters, in common vernacular, are people who dislike, disrespect, and disregard the value and work of a person and make it known by casting dispersion or disdain. The preacher would extrapolate that Paul and Christians had "haters" and then would call to mind that contemporary listeners have haters. The life lesson that the preacher brings forth is summed up as "your haters are your elevators," and this is the thematic focal point of the sermon. Your haters elevate you to your divine destiny.

My problem is that with all of the exegetical gospel texture that is available in this text, the preacher dismisses it or reduces it down and makes the point of how you can overcome your haters, given the fact that they raise you to your "destiny and purpose." This is to minimize the gospel to a weekly life lesson. It is to reduce the opposition and venom that Paul faced in preaching a crucified Lord of glory to a few people on your job who are jealous because you got a raise. It is not possible to give moral equivalence to haters on your job and haters of Paul and the gospel, but when we are looking for a life lesson applicable to the life situation of our hearers, we make such concessions.

Paul even goes so far as to say later, in 1 Corinthians 4:9-13 (NRSV), speaking to the rich about the factional struggles in the Corinthian church, that because of preaching a crucified Lord of glory, the apostles were the refuse and trash of the world:

> For I think that God has exhibited us apostles as last of all, as though sentenced to death, because we have become a spectacle to the world, to angels and to mortals. We are fools for the sake of Christ, but you are wise in Christ. We are weak, but you are strong. You are held in honor, but we in disrepute. To the present hour we are hungry and thirsty, we are poorly clothed and beaten and homeless, and we grow weary from the work of our own hands. When reviled, we bless; when persecuted, we endure; when slandered, we speak kindly. We have become like *the rubbish of the world, the dregs of all things, to this very day.* (italics mine)

We choose "haters are your elevators" because who really wants to hear the gospel of a God who has exhibited Christians as last of all in the parade of a defeated army—last and condemned to die. Who really wants to hear that we suffer for the gospel and are considered as spectacles and the trash, refuse, and garbage of the world? It is difficult to preach this part of the gospel of Christ, and so we settle for a lessening and a cheapening of truth, rather than the unsettling and challenging message of mystery of the gospel.

In this example, the preacher is not really emphasizing the text, but the life lesson of encouragement that she or he believes is pertinent to the congregation. Encouragement is a legitimate concern, and absolutely every one of us needs encouragement; but, in this case, to produce encouragement, looking for the preachable "X," the preacher minimizes Paul and the early church's suffering in the text. This gives the illusion that preachers are preaching the text, but the needs of the people and experience of the preacher is the jumping-off place for the sermon. So, in Farley's terms, preachers preach not the gospel but the Bible, the life lesson of a selected passage. This is a difficult and prophetic challenge to every preacher: just because the preacher is preaching a passage from the Bible does not mean that the gospel is being preached.

For those of us of the African American preaching tradition, I want to add this: just because we "go by the cross" at the close of the sermon every week does not mean that we are preaching the gospel. Going by the cross is the belief that regardless of what text one preaches, one must conclude the sermon with the death, burial, and resurrection of Jesus. Typically, the preacher would detail the events of crucifixion-resurrection narrative, starting with the crucifixion on Friday, the tomb on Friday night, and Jesus in the tomb all night Saturday, and closing with some form of emphasis on the resurrection such as, "Early, bright early, on Sunday morning, Jesus was resurrected with all power in his hands." There are many preachers who think that if another preacher does not "go by the cross," regardless of what that preacher has said, then that preacher has not preached. In its popular form, going by the cross can be formalism, legalism, and—I dare even say—entertainment. Going by the cross must mean presenting the Christ-event in such a way that this past event opens up a new and liberative future in the present. I will say more in the chapter, but we must preach the Christ-event, and not a trope that induces automatic responses to clichés to induce emotional affect from the audience.

In order that we might lower polarization and division, and build a just and more peaceable world, it was important to review several contemporary working gospels in the American context, help preachers to understand that all proclaimers of the gospel have a working gospel, and how

16

very often those working gospels are produced by reading the same biblical text and coming up with very different interpretations. This complexity of various interpretations raises the monumental question that must be responded to in the theology of every preacher: What is the relationship between the Bible and the gospel? How does the Bible function in the preaching of the gospel? In response to this question, Farley introduces us to the bridge paradigm in that the preacher looks looks for the preacheable "X" (life lesson) in the text and abandons the preaching of gospel, such as in the example of our haters being our elevators. In the next chapter, we will explore how the preacher overcomes the bridge paradigm, preaches the mystery of the gospel, and as a matter of integrity set forth my working gospel.

Chapter Two

THE MYSTERY OF THE GOSPEL AND THE PROPHETIC MESSIAH

What happened in Christ was not an exegesis of Scripture… not primarily something that happened in a tradition of textual interpretation. The interpretation of existing Scripture had to limp along as best it could to catch up, and it had no power to annul … the new and unprecedented thing done in Jesus' death and resurrection— that we read and use the Bible in our theological thinking…. What is authoritative is Jesus Christ himself as the Word of God, not a book per se.

—André Resner

O
ne of my standard practices in the preparation of any book is, whenever possible, do public lectures on critical chapters before I finalize them for publication. The feedback from live audiences, versus the audience in my head as I write alone in my study, is rich, fruitful, and a vital source for clarifying thought and improving one's communication skills, both speaking and writing. When I lectured on the first chapter, "The Working Gospel and the Bridge Paradigm," one person asked me if the critique of the life lesson by the bridge paradigm was a little extreme. She suggested that both Farley and I had only highlighted the misuse of the life lesson. Were there not valuable life lessons to be gleaned from the text that were consistent with the exegetical context and did not steer the listener away from the text? It was a very insightful question, and it began

a process of nuanced and balanced evaluation of the bridge paradigm. Many weeks after the initial question, I concluded, with my astute questioner, that we could indeed nuance the bridge paradigm's critique of life lessons by fully exploring Farley's concept of the finitizing of the gospel and preaching the mystery of the gospel. This exploration allows us to get at the heart of Farley's argument. I will begin the chapter concluding the matter of working gospel by demonstration of the working gospel of the Apostle Paul. Then, I will look at the bridge paradigm through the finitizing of the gospel and preaching the mystery of the gospel. As a matter of integrity with the reader, following Luke's working gospel of the prophetic Messiah, I will articulate my own working gospel. I want to look briefly at the working gospel of the Apostle Paul.

Apostle Paul's Working Gospel: The Message of the Cross

L. L. Welborn offers powerful insights on Paul's working gospel in the aforementioned 1 Corinthians 1:18, 22-24 (NIV) text:

> For the message of the cross is foolishness to those who are perishing, but to us who are being saved it is the power of God....Jews demand signs and Greeks look for wisdom, but we preach Christ crucified: a stumbling block to Jews and foolishness to Gentiles,but to those whom God has called, both Jews and Greeks, Christ the power of God and the wisdom of God.

According to Welborn, Paul is specifically and principally addressing the factionalism in the Corinthian church.[1] Some claimed they were of the party of Paul, while others claimed the party of Apollos, the party of Peter, and even the party of Christ. They were openly fighting each other for superiority in the church. To deal with the factionalism, Paul does not discuss theologies, personalities, or philosophies of the contending parties, but more importantly he calls the Corinthians back to the foundation of the gospel, the theology of the cross, the crucified Christ.

---

1. L. L. Welborn, *Paul, the Fool of Christ: A Study of 1 Corinthians 1–4 in the Comic-Philosophic Tradition* (New York: T & T Clark International), 2005.

For Welborn, it is in response to the factionalized situation in Corinth that the language of the "cross" entered into Paul's discourse. Welborn cites that the pre-Pauline kerygmatic formulae in 1 Thessalonians, Paul's earliest epistle, does not contain the word cross at all. In the early years of Paul's mission work and preaching, Jesus's death is not emphasized. It is at the point of Paul's discourse to the Corinthian church that the discourse shifts, and Paul states explicitly the theology of the cross. According to Welborn, Paul invented "a new and more literal Christian discourse," the language of the cross.[2] While discussion of the "cross" in Greco-Roman culture was reserved for gallows humor and jest, and the cruel and disgusting mention of the term was least what the cultured and sophisticated Greco-Romans wanted to hear, Paul redeems "the cross" and regards "the word of the cross" as the whole content of the gospel. The cross that was vulgar and shocking to the elite of Corinth and the upper class was, for Paul and believers, the salvation of the world. From this point on, the central tenet of Paul's discourse is the cross of Christ: "I had made up my mind not to think about anything while I was with you except Jesus Christ, and to preach him as crucified" (2:2). The cross of Christ has become Paul's working gospel. Welborn's assessment of the development of the word of the cross in Paul's working gospel validates our earlier contention in chapter one that one renegotiates one's working gospel and resulting theology based upon the continued reading of scripture and experience of the life of the church and one's own life. Paul's working gospel evolved through time to the gospel of the cross.

I turn now to the major emphasis of the chapter, the balancing and nuancing of Farley's theory of the bridge paradigm by taking a closer look at his understanding of the finitizing of popular religion.

The Finitizing of Popular Religion

My comments from the last chapter on "Your Haters Are Your Elevators" has synergy with an important reflection by Edward Farley on

2. Welborn, *Paul, the Fool of Christ*, 251.

the critical need for preaching to transcend popular religion and piety.[3] Farley defines popular religion or piety as: "the inescapable need to finitize the sacred by identifying it with the ethnocentric, egocentric, and culturally originated beliefs, casuistries, texts, authorities, and emotion-laden certainties of the religious communities."[4] These "finitized" versions of the sacred are often the working gospel that faith communities construct that we discussed in the last chapter as contemporary working gospels. It is very difficult for human beings to grasp the infinite, and in order to establish communication and relationship with the divine, we must make the infinite finite. Popular religion and piety makes God approachable by declaring what God wants, thinks, says, does, or even how God "is." Popular religion and piety, in its inescapability, undergirds every aspect and undertaking of the church and the religious, including, laity, ordained leadership, polity, organizational structures, traditions, worship, sacraments, preaching—everything. No religious community avoids the finitizing of popular religion.

Farley's concern is popular religion and piety can idolatrously equate the infinite God with what human beings do, think, write, say, decide, proclaim, and create. Idolatry occurs when the finite substitutes or equates itself with the infinite. Farley concludes that "authentic faith is not reducible to popular religion" and declares:

> A prophetic, transcendent, and metaphorical aspect, rooted in the fact that the religious community had to do with a sacred Presence is ever at working casting suspicion on popular religion's literalistic tendencies, world constructions, and claims of identity with God.[5]

Popular religion and piety often finds critical expression in preaching. Preaching is an act of authentic faith, and has this intrinsic and abiding tension: "how to voice the convictions of tradition, Scripture, and Gospel in language that finitizes the sacred and at the same time destabilizes that

---

3. Edward Farley, "Sacred Rhetoric: A Practical Theology of Preaching," in *Practicing Gospel: Unconventional Thoughts on the Church's Ministry* (Louisville: John Knox, 2003), 94.

4. Farley, "Sacred Rhetoric," 94.

5. Farley, "Sacred Rhetoric," 94.

language."[6] The only corrective to the idolatry of popular religion and piety is consistent prophetic critique as Resner suggests:

> What needs to happen alongside this idolatrous reductionism is an ongoing prophetic critique of the community's very formulations of faith. Thus faithful communities live in a tension between finiziting reductionism and prophetic exposure of such reductionisms which aim to articulate 'a destabilizing language of mystery.'[7]

A theology of preaching must critique the preaching of popular religion and piety such as "Your Haters Are Your Elevators," and push for the articulation of a destabilizing language of mystery. This is the basis for a critique of every working gospel, including mine, which I will suggest in a few pages. This prophetic critique of the religious community's very formulations of faith will guard against idolatrous reductionism, heresy, and the mix of the Bible with religious and cultural dominance hierarchies that operate so freely and uncritically in popular religion and piety. Farley offers us a mode of prophetic critique necessary for all expressions of working gospels, contemporary, historical, or biblical.

Popular religion and piety, in all of its finitude, must assert that we do not know it all and the mystery of the infinite cannot be fully named. David Jacobsen helps us immeasurably by reminding us of the humility with which we must approach the mystery of the infinite God when he writes:

> Mystery is something *not fully revealed.* . . . We name gospel, rather, in bits and pieces using our best theological reflections because some day God's purposes will be fully revealed. Paul puts it nicely in the KJV: "for now we see through a glass darkly, but then, face to face" (1 Cor. 13:12) Mystery invites our faithful probing and theological brooding, but it is done with profound humility this side of heaven.[8]

---

6. Farley, "Sacred Rhetoric," 95.

7. André Resner, "Reading the Bible for Preaching the Gospel," in *Collected Papers of the 2008 Annual Meeting of the Academy of Homiletics,* paper presented at the annual meeting of The Academy of Homiletics, Boston, MA (December 7, 2008), 220.

8. David Schnasa Jacobsen, "The Practice of Homiletical Theology in a Confessional Mode: An Interim Report on the Homiletical Theology Project," North American Academy of Homiletics meeting in Dallas on December 9, 2017. http://www.bu.edu/homiletical-theology-project.

Jacobsen reminds us that mystery is not a theological escape hatch that we use for sloppy or inadequate thinking. In these matters of working gospel, we would be helped to remember the mystery of the infinite and our profound humility of this side of heaven. The preacher's sacred task is to find words that "bespeak the divine mystery."[9]

The finitizing of popular religion set the stage and takes us another step to nuancing the bridge paradigm.

The Bridge Paradigm and the Mystery of the Gospel

I believe Farley's argument against the bridge paradigm is critical to the preaching of the gospel because it helps preachers discern: (1) what they mean by *gospel*, (2) whether or not the gospel or life lessons are being preached, and (3) whether or not sermons are fostering and forming a gospel-literate congregation as opposed to a congregation of popular religion and piety (i.e., "Your Haters Are Your Elevators"). The ultimate truth and veracity of Farley's argument are vital to the future of preaching, and therefore the goal in this section is the highest and best critical reflection. Some of the most insightful and helpful critique of the bridge paradigm comes from Resner, who makes two important points of critique that I fundamentally agree with.

First, Resner assesses this summary statement by Farley: *The Christian church is summoned to the apostolic task of preaching the gospel, and to preach biblical passages is to reject that summons.*[10] Resner asserts that Farley's claim is "simple (not simplistic) and radical, and in the end confusing. We can all generally agree to the basic premise that the church is called to the apostolic task of preaching the gospel. Farley's difficulty, and ours, comes when he/we attempt to define what is meant by 'the gospel.'" As we said before, we all use the term *gospel*, but we do not all mean the same thing.

---

9. Edward Farley, *Practicing the Gospel: Unconventional Thoughts on the Practice of Ministry* (Louisville: Westminster John Knox, 2004), 101.

10. Farley, *Practicing the Gospel*, 80.

Farley suggests that "the gospel is not a thing to be defined. It is not a doctrine, a delimited objective content."[11] The summaries in Acts and Paul, the formulas of the kerygma, phrases like the "kingdom of God," "Jesus as Lord," "Christ crucified," and so on, have content, "but that content is not simply a quantity of information."[12] As I understand Farley, we try to capture the gospel in language, but the gospel is the Christ-event, the Christ happening, and the Christ experience that is far deeper and more profound than the ability of our language to define it. Farley suggests: "To proclaim [the gospel] means to bring to bear a certain past event on the present in such a way as to open the future. Since the present is always specific and situational, the way that the past, the event of Christ, is brought to bear so as to elicit hope will never be captured in some timeless phrase, some ideality of language."[13] Phrases like "Jesus is Lord" or "Christ crucified" do have meaning, but the question of preaching the good news is how do we express these meanings in practical terms such that the past events of the death and resurrection open up the future of hope and redemptive possibilities in the present. The gospel is "the bringing to bear of the event of Jesus onto the present in such a way that the present is both judged and drawn in hope toward redemption."[14]

The preaching of the apostles—Jesus's life, death, and resurrection—was set in the context of the temporal story of Israel, a past that was transformed by Christ into a new aeon. This means that "salvation through Jesus" is always in direct relationship to the concrete cultural, political, and individual situations in which the preaching takes place. The preacher cannot talk about "salvation through Jesus" as theological content without the location of the theology directly in some community, some flesh-and-blood place, where hearts long for hope and a future. This means, based upon the context of the gospel in a marginalized community, "salvation through Jesus" might look like preaching liberation and justice. On the other hand, based upon the context of the gospel in another community,

---

11. Edward Farley, "Preaching the Bible and Preaching the Gospel," *Theology Today* 51, no. 1 (April 1994): 101.

12. Farley, "Preaching the Bible and Preaching the Gospel," 101.

13. Farley, "Preaching the Bible and Preaching the Gospel," 101.

14. Farley, "Preaching the Bible and Preaching the Gospel," 101.

"salvation through Jesus" may look like focusing exclusively on personal salvation. It is not necessarily the interpretation of "salvation through Jesus," but the call for normativity of one's perspective that is the real issue that slips into cultural dominance hierarchies and oppression.

Farley expresses the specificity and context of the divine word for Israel:

> We recall the prophetic appeal to the exodus deliverance, the covenant, and the Torah. Entangled in these apparently simple terms is a whole cluster of deep symbols concerning justice, community, evil, law, grace, and many other things. 'Salvation through Jesus' retains virtually all of these deep symbols, plus others."[15]

These deep symbols have little meaning if they are not grounded in the experience of a specific community at a specific time. Given this, the gospel is not simply a clear and given content, "the overcoming of sin with a paradigm of redemption based in the Christ event," but also is set in a specific community, at a specific time to have true meaning. [16] The Christ-event with its deep symbols is not able to be neatly coined into phrases, sayings, clichés, and axioms with being contextualized to the needs of a community.

Following Farley, first there was a God event of Christ in the context of the life of a community, then theological reflection occurred to describe the gospel event that happened in the community, and then doctrine occurred to interpret the meaning of the event and fix it in practice in the life of the community. Farley reminds us that the gospel is the mystery of God's salvific work, and, as Paul says, the preachers are the "stewards of the mysteries" (1 Cor 4:1 ASV). Doctrine was never first, the mystery is always first.

Again, when we say the gospel is a mystery, we are not talking about slipshod thinking and foggy esoteric escapes to avoid serious theological issues and questions. Jacobsen reminds us that "mysteries are not merely things we don't *know*, they are things *being revealed*."[17] Because the gospel is a mystery, and is still being revealed, we never master it, exhaust it,

---

15. Farley, "Preaching the Bible and Preaching the Gospel," 102.

16. Farley, "Preaching the Bible and Preaching the Gospel," 102.

17. Jacobsen, "The Practice of Homiletical Theology in a Confessional Mode," 37.

or presume that we comprehend it. Rather, we continue to struggle to fathom its reality. Gospel is not simply given all at once in a formula like a gift-wrapped package, forever understood, perfect, and neat. To fully appreciate the gift in a gift-wrapped package, though the wrapping is part of the gift, one has to tear off the packaging to get at the gift. Likewise, sometimes we must make a mess of the pretty packaging of the content word of the gospel to theologically get at the deepest gift of mystery that is on the inside. Again, Farley says: "It [the gospel] is something to be proclaimed, but the summons to proclaim is a summons to struggle with the mystery of God's salvific action and how that transforms the world. To proclaim the gospel then is to enter the world of the gospel, struggling with questions of suffering, evil, idolatry, hope and freedom."[18]

At this point of Farley's explanation of the gospel, Resner rightly discerns and asks if Farley's explanation is not the bridge paradigm in another form:

> Farley's bridge is *from* a past event *to* a present situation, with the result that the present is opened up.... The Gospel for Farley begins in the past with an event, not a text, but the goal is the same, the bringing to bear of that past event onto the present. To use his own language, in the Farley-bridge paradigm, the preacher's task is to build a bridge from that-which-is-preaching (the God-redemptive event of the past) to the situation of the congregation.[19]

With great insight, Resner names Farley's "real beef" with the bridge paradigm: "the bridge paradigm connects preaching to some fields of theological study, but not to theology."[20] Theological reflection, at best, has not been adequately consulted in the preaching process, and at worst, it has been abandoned. For Farley, generally three fields are consulted to build the bridge paradigm: biblical studies, cultural (sociological and psychological) studies, and rhetorical (communication) studies. We have diminished theological thinking, and Farley believes that "the constructive struggle with truth questions as they pertain to the world of faith, has no place in

[margin note: w/ the ppl of God]

---

18. Farley, "Preaching the Bible and Preaching the Gospel," 102.

19. Resner, "Reading the Bible for Preaching the Gospel," 217.

20. Resner, "Reading the Bible for Preaching the Gospel," 217.

preaching."[21] For Farley, preaching the gospel summons the preacher to theological study and reflection based upon the truth of the text and the issues of suffering, evil, idolatry, hope, and freedom in the world. We enter the world of the gospel by way of the world of the Bible and the world of the interpretation of the Christian faith applied to some concrete situation needing God's intervention.[22] Even so, that which is preached is the gospel and not theology or the Bible. I repeat Jacobsen's reminder from earlier: the preacher is resident theologian and all sermon preparation is theology. Farley asserts the role of theology at the center of the preaching task.

Farley reminds us that we do not preach the conceptual solutions of Tertullian, Aquinas, Augustine, Barth, or Calvin so as to open up the future. We do not preach the Bible, neither do we preach Richard Allen, Martin Luther King Jr., Clarence Jordan, Prathia Hall, James Cone, or Katie Cannon. We miss them all dearly, but we preach "the bringing to bear of the event of Jesus onto the present in such a way that the present is both judged and drawn in hope toward redemption."[23]

Working gospel is an attempt to express the Christ-event, the Christ happening, and locate it in the relevancy of a particular moment and culture. From the hearer's perspective, "the gospel is the mysterious Christ-event that summons believers to faithful existence in the face of whatever happens, whatever is to come."[24] In conclusion of this first point, as I read Farley, he is calling for theological reflection of the Christ-event that opens up redemptive possibilities in the present and future to be the heart of the sermon, not a life lesson that is minimizing of the mystery of the Christ-event.

Now, to the second part of Farley's summary assertion: "the Christian church is summoned to the apostolic task of preaching the gospel and *to preach biblical passages is to reject that summons.*" The second point of critique that Resner makes in regard to Farley's bridge paradigm that I fundamentally agree with is this: far from abandoning the text for the life

---

21. Farley, *Practicing the Gospel,* 82.

22. Farley, "Preaching the Bible and Preaching the Gospel," 102.

23. Farley, "Preaching the Bible and Preaching the Gospel," 101.

24. Farley, "Preaching the Bible and Preaching the Gospel," 101.

lesson as Farley asserts, "most preachers read the Bible with a theological and hermeneutical strategy based upon a working understanding of the Gospel."[25] Resner believes that most preachers do theological reflection unconsciously, and if their sermons were examined over time, one would clearly see a commitment to a "working Gospel." Resner accurately suggests: "Most preachers temper their use of historical criticism by their prior theological commitment to their working gospel, since they are reading the Bible not to write an exegesis paper for an exegesis but to preach the Gospel in the context of a worshipping community."[26]

I agree with Resner that preachers have a working gospel involving a kind of formed theological pre-work before they come to the text and the task of preaching. Theology is involved, and that theology is mostly established in the unconscious working gospel. It could be argued that the theological pre-work does not allow the text to speak for itself, hence the need for ongoing prophetic critique of a working gospel, but there is not an abandonment of theological thinking when the preacher comes to the text.

Though I agree with Resner that often the application of the working gospel in approaching the text is unconscious, the working gospel must be brought to consciousness so that preachers can consistently discern whether they are preaching the gospel or preaching the biblical passage. The working gospel brought to consciousness allows the working gospel to avoid idolatrous reductionism by ongoing prophetic critique of the preacher's and community's very formulations of faith. Preachers can gauge the levels of unhealthy popular religion and/or healthy piety in their sermons and discern if their preaching is weakening or strengthening the quality of gospel literacy in the congregation. I believe that once the working gospel is brought to consciousness, it is possible to garner a life lesson that is true to the context of the text that does not take the listener away from the text. In other words, the bridge paradigm can be an effective mode of preaching if the preacher does the requisite theological reflection on the mystery of the gospel and communicates that the hearer. As we said in the last section, the preacher must "voice the convictions of tradition,

---

25. Resner, "Reading the Bible for Preaching the Gospel," 223.

26. Resner, "Reading the Bible for Preaching the Gospel," 223–24.

Scripture, and Gospel in language that finitizes the sacred and at the same time destabilizes that language."[27]

And finally—preachers must learn to respect other working gospels in order to guard against making their working gospel part of their cultural dominance hierarchy. When we present our working gospel as "the gospel," and thereby seek to make our interpretation normative for all people, we delegitimize the gospel of others, often for cultural reasons. As we bring our own working gospel to conscious level, we have the opportunity to grow in our understanding of our own working gospel and the working gospel of others. It is critical that if we are going to preach dangerous sermons that we be aware of our own working gospel and the working gospel of others.

In the concluding section of this chapter, I will, following Luke, set forth my own working gospel, which is, in Farley's words, "the gospel in its prophetic element—a disruption, an exposure of corporate oppression and individual collusion and uncovering redemptive possibilities."[28] It upsets the dominance hierarchy just as Jesus did in Luke 4:16-30. In concert with Resner, I believe that one of the ways the Christ-event becomes concretely manifest is by shattering all boundaries of ethnicity to become a radially inclusive community.[29] Jesus was led to the cliff by his neighbors for announcing that vision as the prophetic Messiah. He was almost killed for including Gentiles in the divine project. We are often persecuted for the gospel based upon whom we include in heavenly favor.

Luke's Working Gospel: The Prophetic Messiah

I would classify the summary of Jesus's sermon in Luke 4:16-30 as a dangerous sermon. A dangerous sermon is based in the preacher's moral imagination that upends and challenges the dominant moral hierarchy operative in the church and/or cultural context of the preaching event. The dominant

27. Farley, "Sacred Rhetoric," 95.
28. Farley, "Preaching the Bible and Preaching the Gospel," 102.
29. Resner, "Reading the Bible for Preaching the Gospel," 219.

moral hierarchy of the Jewish synagogue was that salvation, based in the expectation of a Jewish messiah, was specifically for the Jews. When Jesus included Gentiles, it stirred antagonism and heated opposition. Let's take a closer look at Luke's working gospel and examine Jesus's dangerous sermon.

Mark, Matthew, and Luke all tell of an episode in Jesus's hometown in which his sermon is rejected by his familial neighbors (Matt 13:54-58 and Mark 6:1-6a). In Mark and Matthew, the conflicted incident is set at a time later in the ministry of Jesus. Jesus's hometown people are amazed that Jesus, whose origin and upbringing they know firsthand, could exhibit such tremendous wisdom and power. They ask, "Isn't this the carpenter's son?" They mention that they are familiar with the whole family—Joseph, Mary, and the sisters and brothers of Jesus. Then, they take offense at him and ask, "Where did he get all these things?" Jesus responds by saying that a prophet has no honor in his own hometown. Because of their lack of faith, Jesus could not do many miracles. Mark especially mentions that Jesus was amazed at their lack of faith. Luke's working gospel expands Mark's version and places the sermon at the beginning of Jesus's ministry. Luke's purpose is to establish this as the inaugural sermon and the programmatic cornerstone of Jesus's ministry.

The text in Luke opens in verse 4:14 (ASV) by mentioning that Jesus, "in the power of the Spirit," returns to Galilee. The term "power of the Spirit" is a reference to the powerful affirmation Jesus received from heaven in the waters of baptism with John the Baptist (Luke 3:21-28). Coming up out of the water of baptism, the Spirit drives Jesus into the desert to be tempted and tested by the devil (Luke 4:1-13). When the temptations are finished, Jesus begins a ministry of itinerant teaching, and the text in verse 14 (NRSV) says, "a report about him spread through all the surrounding country." He teaches in their synagogues and everyone praises him. Jesus makes an itinerant teaching circuit of local communities. Eventually, he comes home to Nazareth, to his family, friends, and the community that raised him. The Lukan text in verse 16 says that he goes to synagogue, as is his custom. Synagogues were the religious, social, and educational nucleus of Jewish community, akin to what we might call an assembly hall, auditorium, or worship center. Synagogues functioned as community centers, guesthouses, and even schools for children. Synagogues could be understood as a gathering place and could be established with ten or more males over the age of thirteen. Torah was read and expounded at synagogue.

The official in charge was called the "ruler of the synagogue." Scholars say the role functioned perhaps as librarian, worship committee, custodian, and schoolteacher. The ruler did not preach or expound Torah, and therefore Sabbath teaching and exposition fell to the laity and, on this occasion, to Jesus.

The scripture was read from a standing position. Jesus stands, and the scroll of the prophet Isaiah is given to him. Jesus unrolls the scroll, finds Isaiah 61:1-2 (NRSV), and reads:

> The Spirit of the Lord God is upon me,
>> because the Lord has anointed me
>> to bring good news to the poor.
> He has sent me to proclaim release to the captives
>> and recovery of sight to the blind,
>> and to let the oppressed go free,
>> to proclaim the year of the Lord's favor.[30]

Jesus rolls up the scroll, gives it back to the attendant, and sits down. The congregation would have seen that as a sign for the beginning of a teaching, an interpretation of the text just presented, and therefore, their eyes were fixed upon him. No extended sermon of explanation ensues, or perhaps Luke only includes the summary, but Jesus declares in Luke 4:21: "Today, this scripture has been fulfilled in your hearing."

The congregation is amazed. Jesus declared himself the fulfillment of the prophetic scripture, the Messiah, the long-awaited one for the deliverance of Israel. There can be no question: Jesus is the Messiah. What until now had been potential, promise, and hope for the arrival of the Messiah, is a present reality and is fulfilled. The Messiah had come.

---

30. Upon close inspection of the Septuagint version of Isaiah 61:1-2, the phrase "binding up the brokenhearted" has been omitted from the original text, and a line from Isaiah 58:6—"to let the oppressed free"—has been added. Jesus stops at the textual reference to the day of vengeance of our God and ends with "the year of the Lord's favor" (NABRE).

What did this declaration of the coming of the Messiah mean? How would the synagogue audience interpret the messianic declaration? What kind of Messiah is Jesus? One scholar convincingly argues that by quoting Isaiah, Jesus builds on the imagery of the Jubilee year mandated in Leviticus 25:23-55. Every fifty years, Israel was to declare a "year of liberty," based upon God's prior action of liberation in freeing them from slavery and hard labor in Egypt. The year of liberty was to be marked by four types of required rest or relief: (a) the land would be granted a year of rest, a "fallow" year when no crops would be sown; (b) debts would be cancelled; (c) any indentured servant would be set free; and (d) any ancestral lands that were sold out of financial necessity (the only conceivable way that you would sell ancestral lands) would be returned to those to whom God had originally allocated them when the Israelites entered the land.

The actual implementation of the year of Jubilee would result in periodic and vast economic disruption and upheaval. Practically, the Jubilee laws would have prevented the accumulation of wealth—particularly capital in the form of land—from accumulating in any one single family's hands. Rather, once in a lifetime, the entire economy would be given a fresh start. History gives no evidence that a Jubilee year ever was celebrated. Sharon H. Ringe suggests, "It would seem likely that so thoroughgoing economic and social restructuring would have been noted somewhere. If it had been observed, such a year would have surely have been consternation among those whose investments would have been threatened."[31] Such disruption was very difficult, if not impossible, based upon human political, economic, and social interests. But from Jesus's perspective, this is exactly the point. Jubilee is only possible by the proclamation of the in-breaking reign of God. The year of Jubilee represented a titanic shift in allegiance from loyalties to the systems and structures of the temporal human order to a new participation in God's reign of justice and peace. The prophet is a herald trumpeting the year of God's favor and liberty. These words from Isaiah, in both the time of the exile during Isaiah's ministry and Jesus's time of Roman occupation in Palestine, were tremendous comfort and promise. God has good news for the poor, a future of healing

---

31. Sharon H. Ringe, *Luke* (Louisville: John Knox, 1995), 69.

and release from various and all forms of captivity. In Jesus's presence and preaching of the year of Jubilee, the new order of promise has taken on human flesh and has been fulfilled, "today."

In this Lukan version, the hometown audience asks, "Is this Joseph's son?" The exact tone of their question is difficult to interpret. Their question could be neutral, admiring, skeptical, or some mixture of all. It could be an expression of wonder and marvel or an expression of dismissal and doubt. It could be thankful that the Messiah has now come or how dare he presume to rise above his circumstances and make all these grand promises, after all we know his people and his humble beginnings.

What is clear in Luke is how Jesus interpreted their comments. He took them as expressive of admiration with deep skepticism. He says to them: "Surely you will say—physician—heal thyself" (Luke 4:23), and "prophets are not accepted in their hometown" (Luke 4:24). He makes clear the declaration of the text has been fulfilled and is true, and he does not pacify them. He challenges them in the full expansiveness of the reign of God based in the fact that the "year of the Lord's favor" would not be quite what they expected.

Jesus refers to Elijah's healing of the widow of Zarepath and Elisha's healing of Naaman (1 Kings 17:8-9 and 2 Kings 5:14 respectively). These prophets perform their healing acts among Gentiles and not exclusively for Israelites alone. The healing work of Elijah and Elisha did touch Israel, but it began outside the Jewish community. Ringe suggests, "Luke 4:25-27 portrays Jesus telling the townspeople that their longing for evidence of the fulfillment of which he spoke might well not come to them first of all. They have no priority of place, and, as John had warned earlier (3:8), no basis on which to claim privilege in this divine project."[32]

The anger and wrath of the hometown family, friends, and relatives explode. They drove him to the hill such as to represent ridding the city of defilement, as if he were a plague or were speaking of the blasphemous worship of foreign gods. We would know them as a lynch mob. The sermon of this native son violently offended them at the core of their faith. It was a dangerous sermon, and they wanted to kill him for it.

---

32. Ringe, *Luke*, 70.

Jewish hearers believed that they had the inside track, but in Jesus's sermon, the presumption that salvation is the exclusive right of Jews is revoked. Most Jews identified themselves as the poor and oppressed, and in the text, favor is being bestowed upon Israel. The *New Pillar Commentary* suggests: "By identifying Gentiles as models of faith in a sermon to Jews, Jesus made the revolutionary point that salvation is not limited for Jews, but also includes Gentiles. The sermon in Nazareth effectively anchors the Gentile mission, not in the later conversion of Cornelius (Acts 10), as often supposed, but in the initial proclamation of the gospel by Jesus himself."[33] Luke is suggesting that the extension of the gospel to Gentiles in Acts 10 was not an afterthought because Jews rejected Jesus. It was the result of divine election of Gentiles, already operative in the days of Elijah and Elisha, and indeed, even in the days of Abraham, who at the time was called a Gentile (Gen 11–12). They could not hear this painful truth: that if they did not affirm salvation for the Gentiles, then they could not affirm it for themselves. In this atmosphere of anger, rage, hostility, and venom at the edge of a cliff, the text is clear no harm comes to Jesus. The text of Luke 4:30 says that he walks right through the crowd and goes his way. Luke is clear that Jesus's agenda, mission, and work are established. Jesus is the prophetic Messiah. This is Luke's working gospel.

Jesus continues God's liberating work through exorcisms, healings, and teachings of the people. According to Luke Timothy Johnson, "The radical nature of his mission as the prophetic messiah is inaugurated by its offer and acceptance by those who were the exiles, outsiders, lepers, castaways, marginalized: the prophetic messiah is available to all outcasts everywhere."[34] Salvation is available for the poor and oppressed of all nations and of all times, and not just for Jews.

The prophetic Messiah and the years of the Lord's favor even reach down to chattel slaves and their descendants in the contemporary United States of America. It is for this reason that I have accepted Luke's prophetic Messiah and adopted this gospel of liberation as my working gospel. By

---

33. James R. Edwards, *The New Pillar Commentary: The Gospel According to Luke* (Grand Rapids: Eerdmans, 2015), 132–33.

34. Luke Timothy Johnson, *The Gospel of Luke,* Sacra Pagina Series (Collegeville, MN: Liturgical Press, 1991), 81.

virtue of the reign of God inaugurated in this Lukan text, I was included and accepted the prophetic Messiah.

Sometimes in my preaching, I tell the insiders that salvation will not come to them first, but to those outside and far off. It is dangerous when you tell insiders that without affirming the salvation of whomever their community categorizes as outsiders—such as whites, blacks, same-gender-loving people, Democrats, Republicans, men, women, the poor, immigrants, gun rights activists, convicts, abortion doctors, the rich, or rappers—that they cannot affirm their own salvation. Sometimes it does not go well. History is full of courageous people who spoke to belligerent crowds, and every now and then, a preacher might take the risk to preach the gospel and do the same.

At the end of the dangerous sermon, Jesus was on the verge of being thrown off the cliff by his hometown crowd. What prompted this response was that Jesus preached out of his moral imagination, proclaimed the fulfillment of the year of Jubilee, and upset the prevailing dominance hierarchy. In this instance, the reign of God that Jesus proclaimed made all people equal servants, evidenced by the fact that God made salvation possible to Gentiles. Jesus upended the dominance hierarchy of the Roman Empire, Jewish religion, and the Jewish synagogue. In fact, he was crucified and killed for preaching dangerous sermons. But thanks be to God that the dominance hierarchy of the world does not have the final say. The resurrection is testimony that God will have the last word, and the moral orders of the world will become the moral order of our Christ. This prophetic Messiah and Paul's crucified Christ is the heart of my working gospel.

For all of us who herald the prophetic Messiah and were metaphorically taken to our own cliff to be thrown off, there is this as a sign of hope. In verses 31-32, Jesus leaves Nazareth, goes down to Capernaum, and begins to teach the people, and they were amazed at his teaching and said, "his message had authority." There are other audiences that will be receptive of the message.

In the effort to help preachers understand different moral worldviews, and to help them better understand their own worldviews, I want to turn to the unconscious moral worldview and the work of George Lakoff.

Chapter Three

Chapter Three

THE UNCONSCIOUS MORAL WORLDVIEW AND THE DANGEROUS SERMON

Most of our thought is unconscious—not unconscious in the Freudian sense of being repressed, but unconscious simply in that we are not aware of it. We think and talk at too fast a rate and too deep a level to have conscious awareness of everything we think and say. We are even less aware of components of thought—concepts. When we think, we use an elaborate system of concepts, but we are not usually aware of just what those concepts are like and how they fit together in a system. That is what I study: what, exactly, our unconscious system is and how we think and talk using a system of concepts.

—George Lakoff

In the last chapter, I explored both André Resner's theory of working gospel and Edward Farley's critique of the bridge paradigm, and definition of the mystery of the gospel. I encouraged those who would preach dangerous sermons to be aware of their own working gospel, and to be cognizant, as best as one can, of the working gospel of the audience to whom one preaches. The danger of exclusively privileging one's working gospel is the tendency to diminish the working gospel of others, and even label them "illegitimate." This easily connects with cultural dominance hierarchies in which our beliefs, worldview, and politics amalgamate with our own working gospel and offer religious sanction to our privilege. Farley reminds us that the gospel is a mystery, and the fullness of its truth is not yet fully revealed. Mystery invites our theological brooding with a profound sense of humility. It is only humility that allows us to respect the working gospel of those who we do not agree with.

In this second chapter, I want to explore the insights from the field of cognitive science through the work of distinguished professor of cognitive science and linguistics, George Lakoff.[1] In view of my desire to utilize Lakoff's understanding of dual and competing moral orders as means to help survive a dangerous sermon, I want to begin with three critical assertions: first, preachers must understand their own moral worldview and how that worldview shapes and influences the theology and working gospel that guides their preaching. If preachers do not understand their own moral order, they have no reliable basis to ascertain the moral order of the audience to whom they speak and the dangerous sermon becomes a shot in the dark.

Second, if we understand and accept the reality of different moral worldviews, we can rhetorically shape the dangerous sermon in the manner that gives it the best chance to be heard. Many times we preach dangerous sermons with little understanding of an opposing moral order and initiate resistance and often antagonism that might could have better managed if we understood differing moral orders.

Third, if preachers understood different moral orders, those preachers are in the best position to help a congregation understand moral orders that they might not agree with, be familiar with, or normally demonize and not associate with. One of the critical roles of preachers who desire reconciliation and understanding between people rather than division and polarization is that the preacher must educate audiences to respect different moral orders. Some congregations are made up of predominantly one moral order, while many congregations are mixed with conservatives, liberals, independents, moderates, unaffiliated, and, as we will soon learn, Strict Father and Nurturant Parent moralists. The goal of the preacher

---

1. George Lakoff, *Moral Politics: How Liberals and Conservatives Think*, 3rd ed. (Chicago: University of Chicago Press, 2016).

interested in reconciliation is the same: help congregants become familiar with a different moral order.

The result of these aforementioned three assertions is a certain moral order dexterity that offers the preacher the agility to go well beyond glib usage of labels, stereotypes, tribal tropes, prejudices, divisive language, and especially demonization. The preacher who is aware of different moral orders has the ability to develop sermons that educate, inspire, and invite people beyond unintentional divisive rhetoric and polarizations.

The Nation as Family Metaphor

Following the "nation as a family metaphor," Lakoff postulates two diverse views of reality based in two distinct moral imaginations operating in American culture: the "Strict Father morality" of conservatives and the "Nurturant Parent morality" of progressives. A significant number of people in this nation adhere to Strict Father morality, while a substantial number of others follow Nurturant Parent morality. Independents and moderates tend to be more fluid and go back and forth between both moral orders depending on the presenting issue. These diverse worldviews often clash in the political, economic, social, and religious arenas of American life and, for reasons too numerous and complex to go into here, have generated huge division, polarization, and demonization.[2]

In the first section of this chapter, I want to delve briefly into Lakoff's general discussion of cognitive science and the unconscious. Next, I will explore Strict Father and Nurturant Parent moralities by introducing you to model citizens of each—John and Kathy—who might be members of any congregation, sitting on any pew, on any average Sunday in America.

---

2. Many find the majority of the discussion centered around conservatives and liberals restricting, and they quickly suggest that it does not apply to them or many of their friends, congregational members, or classmates. Both liberalism and conservativism are tremendously diverse, and many do not fit easily into such monolithic categories. Not to mention that more and more people are calling themselves independent to overcome the limitations of conservatism and liberalism. I again acknowledge to the reader that there are wide swaths of variation, and trying to deal with this diversity takes us well beyond the scope of a concise discussion. Lakoff admits just this when he says these categories of conservatism and liberalism exhibit "a great many variations on the central case" of conservatives and liberals. (See Lakoff, *Moral Politics*, 284). For purposes of discussion, we are discussing the central case.

Chapter Three

By way of John and Kathy, I will survey broad generalizations of the dual moral orders and even discuss the ability of each moral order to demonize the other. I will close the chapter with a brief discussion of implications for preaching the dangerous sermon: how we must both hold on to what we believe and bridge to a different moral order.

I believe Lakoff's model of the nation as family and the dual moral orders that follow help the preaching of the dangerous sermon, when possible, to make understandable arguments and bridge into another moral worldview. My hope is that dangerous sermons move congregants to reduce division, polarization, and demonization in the American social, political, and religious landscape by the minimization of inadvertent and contentious rhetoric and schism.

Parenthetically, I must make the reader aware that I am going to discuss the traditional conservative position. With the candidacy and presidency of Donald J. Trump, conservatism has morphed and changed drastically. Based upon recent policy decisions relative to traditional conservative issues such as small government, reducing the national debt, and constitutional conservatism, traditional conservative principles have been jettisoned. A discussion of this Trump revolution is outside of the scope of this book and will take us far off the subject. Therefore, I have chosen to stick with what most know as traditional conservatism, not knowing if traditional conservatism will ever come back as a significant force in American life. Let's look at Lakoff's view of the cognitive science and the unconscious.

Cognitive Science and the Unconscious

Cognitive scientists such as Lakoff believe that only a tiny amount of our thought is actually conscious, with typical estimates that only 2 percent is conscious and 98 percent is unconscious. Unconscious thought is the object of study in the field of cognitive science, and Lakoff argues that

40

moral worldviews are typically unconscious. Lakoff makes a critical point about how our brains work unconsciously:

> Inputs from the senses presented to the eyes, ears or touch take about a tenth of a second before they become conscious. That is so fast for conscious thinking that we do not notice any difference between the input to the sense and our conscious perception. Neurons fire at one thousandth of a second, and take three to five one thousandth of a second to fire again. It takes many neurons and a sequence of neural firings to take sense input and turn it into conscious perception. *In that time, it is common for the visual, sound, or touch system to make a change, cancelling out part of what is present to the senses and creating a new input that fits the circuitry already in the brain. This also happens with facts that do not fit one's worldview.*[3]

We can fit new information or discordant information to our worldview into already formatted neural circuitry. The result is that our brains can re-route or cancel out information that does not synchronize with our worldview, and one of several things can happen:

Facts may be changed to fit our worldview.

Facts may be ignored.

Facts may be rejected and possibly ridiculed.

Facts threatening to our worldview may be attacked.

For Lakoff, the dismissing of facts that do not fit our worldview is what happens most frequently in political discourse today. Deep and persisting moral worldviews tend to be part of our brain circuitry and become part of our identity. The more a neural "idea-circuit" is used in the brain, the stronger it gets, and may eventually become permanent and effectively hard-wired. It is particularly difficult when moral views become part of our identity because when presented with new information, especially information that conflicts with our worldview, we have to change who we understand ourselves to be to accept the information. In most cases, the

---

3. Lakoff, *Moral Politics*, xii–xiii (italics added).

neural wiring and identity stays, and the facts are ignored, dismissed, ridiculed, or attacked.

With information of the hard-wiring of the moral worldview in the neural "idea-circuit" of the brain, it is clear how difficult it is to change one's understanding of one's identity. Lakoff suggests, "It takes extraordinary openness, training, and awareness of this phenomena [neural hard-wiring] to pay critical attention to the vast number of facts we are presented with each day" such that we might be open to change.[4] For the vast majority of the general public, and those in politics, media, and religion, our neural "idea-circuit" becomes permanently hard-wired, our identities fixed, and we believe that our worldview is reality.

Lakoff gives two very interesting and excellent examples of the dismissal of daily facts. The first is the conservative view that totally mystifies progressives: the denial of global warming. For progressives, in the face of massive amounts of scientific evidence, proof, and fact, and the images of melting glaciers and droughts, fires, floods, natural disasters, and record temperatures, it seems to be the height of absurdity and irrationality to deny climate change. Lakoff reminds us that no normal person will consciously admit that they are denying scientific facts. Instead, our brains do the work and automatically and unconsciously censure the information that goes to the brain such as to produce the effect of science denial. Therefore, it makes all the sense in the world to conservatives that climate change is a farce in the face of overwhelming scientific evidence.

The second example of the dismissal of fact is the deeply held belief by many progressives that presentation of facts will automatically lead to the right conclusion. This is the worldview of the centuries-old view of rationality and reason, a worldview that is at odds with cognitive and brain sciences. This worldview believes that all people have the same basic logic and, if presented with the same set of facts, will draw, as rational animals, similar conclusions. If it is true that most thought is unconscious, then facts are only addressing 2 percent of the brain that is conscious and not addressing 98 percent that is unconscious where the hard-wired moral worldview resides. The unconscious works by, as Lakoff suggests,

---

4. Lakoff, *Moral Politics*, xiii.

"embodied primitive frames, conceptual metaphor, and conceptual integration."[5] In our contemporary time, year after year, progressives keep telling facts to conservative audiences with little result. In Lakoff's view, progressives deny the reality of cognitive science as much as conservatives deny the reality of climate change. Both are engaging in a form of science denial based upon a moral worldview hard-wired in the brain.

The practical result of this is that from their worldview, many progressives have a low opinion of conservatives, considering them to be uninformed, stupid, greedy, mean, or just plain crazy. Conservatives despise the "educated liberal elite," who, because of their education and humanism, in their arrogance and pride, look down their noses at average and uneducated people. Therefore, many conservatives support anti-intellectual bias in the attempt to combat "liberal bias." On the whole, conservatives, independents, moderates, and progressives are normal people who happen to have a moral worldview deeply embedded in their brains, whose personal identity is significantly defined by that moral order, and as a result, who become deeply resistant to growth and change that does not fit their worldview.

In this world of fake news, alternative facts, and discussions as to whether truth and facts can ever be known, this is absolutely important to clarify: Lakoff is not suggesting that facts do not matter. His meaning is that facts "have to be framed in appropriately moral terms so that they can be taken seriously."[6] As I understand Lakoff, the question is, How does one make understandable arguments from one moral worldview that might appeal to another moral worldview? If we argue from our worldview into another worldview on our moral terms, it might be that the brain of the other worldview deletes our arguments. If I am going to preach a dangerous sermon, how do I construct arguments that build a bridge so that another worldview and I can communicate? This is Lakoff's main point: regardless of whether we are speaking to an audience made up of progressives, independents, conservatives, or moderates,

---

5. Lakoff, *Moral Politics*, xiv.

6. Lakoff, *Moral Politics*, xv.

"to be understood, one has to place the facts within the worldview of the audience."[7]

Lakoff quickly adds a note of caution in attempting to bridge to another worldview: one must ascertain whether the audience is made up of hardcore believers, bi-conceptuals, or pragmatic moderates in order to have any chance of being heard. My experience is that hardcore believers are very difficult—if not impossible—to convince. There is very little, if anything, that one can say to overcome the hard-wiring in the brain and convince hardcore believers. Case closed. What Lakoff calls bi-conceptuals, or pragmatic moderates, are more open to discussions that might lead to understanding another worldview. Therefore, it might be that our arguments in our dangerous sermons are aimed at bi-conceptuals or pragmatic moderates on both sides. It is useless to appeal to someone who refuses to be open to persuasion.

I want to introduce you to John as an exemplar of the Strict Father morality of the conservative worldview.

John as the Model Citizen of the Conservative Worldview

John is forty-six years old and grew up in a strict household. Now that he is married with two children, he runs his household exactly as his authoritarian father did, despite protesting in his youth that he would not do so in a million years. Without question, the man is the head of the house, and women and children must submit to his authority. He is responsible for the moral order of the family, and his role is to instill discipline, self-responsibility, and self-reliance in the family, especially in the children. These are key ethical values, and without them, it is impossible to be successful in life.

When kids depart from the household discipline and rules of order, he strictly enforces adherence with punishment. He believes the best way to motivate is through rewards and punishments. There are rewards for adhering to discipline, and wherever there is non-adherence, punishment is the best

7. Lakoff, *Moral Politics*, xv.

teacher. *If the children are not disciplined and, therefore, not moral, they become like poor people, who deserve their poverty because, for the most part, they are lazy. The best people are disciplined and prosperous and win in the world.*

He believes in meritocracy and that a lack of moral strength makes one immoral. If people are not successful, it is their own fault because they have broken a moral code—that is, laziness, addiction, low levels of skill and competencies, dependence on handouts, and so on. He believes he has the absolute right to keep what he has made because he earned it by his own merit.

John's success is evidence and proof that the moral order he reinforces is true. He worked his way up from the bottom, and no one ever gave him handouts. He succeeded through disciplined hard work and sheer effort and abhors government handouts. In his view, he has accumulated great wealth because of his moral strength (discipline, self-responsibility, and self-reliance). He is doggedly against the government either restricting his business or subjecting him to taxes, especially to benefit "freeloaders." He fashions himself a "wealth creator," and based upon his wealth creation, he makes possible the wealth of many other "takers" by supplying jobs. He is philanthropic and supports many community and religious causes, which are also supported by other like-minded people. He is against government healthcare, supports the criminal justice system and the police, and advocates for strict "law and order."

He believes he was born in the greatest country the world has ever seen. His ancestors came to this land as freedom-loving heroes and dealt fairly with Indians and Mexicans. He cannot say that about America's dealings with blacks, but much of that is in the past, and he cannot take responsibility for the past. America is a "land of opportunity," and everyone can pull themselves up by their own bootstraps regardless of past treatment. He believes that all this discussion of race, gender, ethnicity, sexual preference, and religious difference is a form of identity politics that divides rather than unifies people. He is nostalgic about the pre-1960s and the post-World War II 1950s when, he says, "things were much simpler."

He believes in the strict maintenance of borders and a strong military to protect from external evils. American protective actions are moral and inhibiting them is immoral. The moral order of conservatism defines legitimate

45

authority and he is sworn to uphold it. Anyone who goes against this moral order is immoral. He goes to church on a regular basis and believes God has ordained the moral order he has benefited from. He loves to hear sermons upholding the conservative moral order and believes the preacher should not spend time in church on political or social issues, but the gospel of Jesus Christ that saves souls. John will not often say it but believes it: you can tell who are the most moral by who won. He is a winner. God helps and blesses those who win.

John is an example of the model citizen of Strict Father morality: those who tend to be successful, wealthy, law-abiding, conservative businesspeople, who support a strong military and a strict criminal justice system, who are against government regulation, and who are definitely against affirmative action. Through their success and wealth, they create jobs, by which they "give" wealth to other citizens. They also, by their philanthropy, voluntarily give to many charitable organizations and causes for the good of the community. These model citizens have been given nothing by the government and made it on their own. They are testimonies to the American dream: any honest, self-disciplined, hard-working person can accomplish the same. According to conservative moral order, all citizens should emulate and be like John.

John clearly wholeheartedly believes in what we mentioned in the introduction as the conservative dominance hierarchy. Lakoff established the following dominance hierarchy that flows from the Strict Father morality of conservatives and generates a large portion of conservative political policies: "God over Human Beings; Human beings over Nature; Adults over Children; the Rich over the Poor (and hence, Employers over Employees); Western Culture over Non-Western Culture; Our Country over Other Countries...Men over Women; Whites over Nonwhites; Straights over Gays; Christians over Non-Christians."[8] We said that dominance hierarchy often functions to explain and justify position and rank in the moral order: people at the top justifiably rule, and the people at the bottom rightly follow. The dominance hierarchy limits the freedom of those lower on the hierarchy by legitimating the power of those higher on the hierarchy. Practically speaking, the most moral are at the top of the

---

8. Lakoff, *Moral Politics*, 413.

freedom, resource, and legitimacy food chain and the least moral are at the bottom. The people at the top are "winners" and have authority, assets, and legitimacy, while people at the bottom are "losers" with limited capacity to share in the resources of freedom, power, and wealth.

I will return to this dominance hierarchy in the latter part of this chapter, but it is clear for John that he is of the group that is the most disciplined and the most moral and therefore should rule. This is at the heart of conservative worldview. Winners are the most moral, and their success is evidence of their discipline. This also means that if you are not successful, you are not disciplined, and not being disciplined will cause you to lose in life, and it is completely the fault of the undisciplined. Blaming social and societal factors, such as background, upbringing, or neighborhood, is nothing but making excuses for moral failure.

Part of the value of Lakoff's work is that, if taken seriously, it illumines and hopefully disposes of worldview myths about people of a differing worldview and makes space for respecting differences by the destruction of hard-wired caricatures and stereotypical associations of each worldview. As an example, and particularly relevant while we are discussing conservative values, Lakoff dispels the myth that conservatives are not compassionate people and labels them "in-group nurturants." They principally nurture and are compassionate to people in their own community who have their values. If someone is outside of their metaphoric family or community, they generally feel less inclined to provide help. Many Americans see enormous differences between Americans subject to disasters who share their values and those who do not. The in-group nurturant behavior can be summed up in this motto: do unto others only if they share your values.

In-group nurturant behavior often gets expressed in an individual orientation at the level of individual help, individual responsibility, and individual care. Conservatives are suspicious of government help and anything that is not voluntary action because when government help is forced, some people might get help that does not uphold their group values. They want to be generous when they want to be and not because the government tells them they have to be or their government taxes force them to be.

In summary, here are **Key Principles of the Conservative Worldview and Strict Father Morality:**

- Life is difficult and competitive, and the world is a fundamentally dangerous place; self-discipline is how to survive.

- Success is a sign of obedience and self-discipline in a competitive world.

- Meritocracy: some are better off in the world and deserve to be based upon their obedience and discipline. They deserve to have authority over others and their authority is legitimate.

- The rich deserve their wealth and those who are poor, either through lack of industry or talent, deserve their poverty. Either they did not work hard enough, were slothful, or were not talented enough, and naturally they deserve their lower rank.

- If moral people have the discipline to just say no to sex or drugs and support themselves in this land of opportunity, then they avoid failure because failure is also due to moral weakness (for example, immorality, poverty, and having children outside of marriage can be explained as moral weaknesses).

- Any discussion of social causes cannot be relevant because the issue is individual morals, not social forces.

Key words encapsulating values of Strict Father morality are **discipline, authority, order, boundaries, homogeneity, purity, and self-interest.** John is sitting on the average pew, in the average church, on the average Sunday in America.

By way of contrast, I want to introduce to Kathy as an exemplar of Nurturant Parent morality.

Kathy as the Model Citizen of the Progressive Worldview

Kathy is a thirty-seven-year-old woman who has never been married. She is raising teenage twins—one girl and one boy—whom she had as an unwed mother when she was twenty years old. She was working on her associate degree at the time of her pregnancy, and with the help of parents, friends, and temporary government assistance, she both gave birth to healthy babies and finished her degree. She trained to be a dental assistant and has worked for the same dentist for twenty years. For the last eight years, she has managed the entire office.

One of her main values is empathy, and she defines it as caring for others and caring for herself. She has compassion for those who need help because she received so much help from family and friends in raising her children. She believes there are many people who cannot help and protect themselves and considers it immoral for a government of the people, by the people, and for the people not to provide temporary help for the people. Her mantra is: life is so fragile that we do not know who will need help, so we help, because sooner or later, it will be us.

She also takes very good care of herself. She eats healthy, watches her weight, and has regular physical checkups and screenings. She negotiated with the insurance provider to provide assistance with health club memberships for the dental office staff, and she leads by example by working out three times per week. Empathy and compassion for others and herself are at the heart of her moral order.

She wants both of her children to be able to take care of themselves, make responsible decisions, and be creative, communicative, and fair. She believes that if she respects her children, then they will respect her. She believes in open communication with them, involving them in decisions. She is accountable to them and they are accountable to her. As a parent, she has the final say but wants the children involved so they can see how decisions are made and learn to make quality decisions. Authority is gained by trust, honesty, and transparent involvement. Obedience comes out of love and respect for the parent(s), not out of fear and punishment. She believes administering fear and punishment to motivate runs dangerously close to abuse.

She empathizes deeply with others and wants people to be treated fairly. She worries about excessive force by police in the case of her son and lack of women's rights and equal pay for her daughter. When her children further their education, she sees them racking up life-altering debt. She does not necessarily believe in free education but believes there must be another alternative

49

to the future shackling debt of so many children. She has accumulated a fair amount of wealth according to middle-class standards. She has a 401(k) plan and savings outside of Social Security. She believes the strength of America is its diversity. She values multiculturalism and the significance of everyone's culture and religion. She has faith in the concept of the common good of all, and if individual good does not contribute to the common good, then it is no good.

She wonders why the nation cannot achieve common-sense gun control. She wants access to healthcare for all. She wants something done about climate change. And while she understands that we must control our borders, she also believes that people should be treated humanely. She is pro-choice and respects a woman's right to choose. She believes that people who are LGBTQI should have all the rights of every other tax paying citizen. She attends a church that promotes a social justice agenda. The gospel of Jesus Christ saves the souls and the neighborhoods of so many without privilege. Based on her faith, she wants her preacher to speak to the relevant issues of the time, and not just about issues of personal faith. The gospel of Jesus Christ addresses social issues and she wants to hear thoughtful sermons from the Bible addressing social concerns, such as poverty, mass incarceration, racism, gun control, universal access to healthcare, and climate change. From her perspective, if God and the church do not address these issues, then what is the point of religion? She is an advocate of the social justice gospel.

Kathy is an example of the model citizen of Nurturant Parent morality: those who value empathy and compassion and want to see defense spending reduced and more money directed to social programming that benefits people such as healthcare, upgrading the school system, job training, and so on. Corporations are to be regulated, lest they misuse and abuse average people as they often do when they buy the political process with money and lobbyists. Wealth is created by the hard work of people in the system, and society has a right to claim part of the wealth that is made. The American dream is difficult for some to achieve because some have advantages and others do not. The playing field for the American dream must be leveled.

For Kathy, empathy is to project your consciousness onto another person. It is to feel what another feels. If one wants to feel a sense of well-being, one wants others to experience the same sense of well-being and therefore has the responsibility to help others achieve well-being. Empathy is the responsibility for helping people even when those people have different values than your own. Empathy sees the world through the eyes of another and, for the most part, finds it hard to demonize people. Nurturant empathy can be summed up in this maxim: do unto others as you would have them do unto you. According to the progressive worldview, all citizens should emulate and be like Kathy.

Nurturants believe that children who receive loving and mutual interaction become responsible, self-disciplined, and self-reliant adults. Obedience comes out of love and respect for the parents and not out of dominance, fear, and punishment. Children do not learn through rewards and punishments. Nurturants do not believe in corporal punishment and violence, because violence begets violence. If children learn that abuse, punishment, and violence are ways to impose authority and respect, they will produce abuse, punishment, and respect and we will have a violent world. Though parents make the final decision, all family members participate in important decisions. Nurturant parents are more likely to practice equally sharing responsibilities between spouses, if there is a spouse. The parental objective is to raise children who have the ability to take care of themselves and nurture others

In summary, here are **Key Principles of the Progressive Worldview and Nurturant Parent Morality:**

- Those who are weak and need help get it from the strong basic bonds of affection, respect, and interdependence.

- Nurturance provided by the natural environment must be sustained.

- Children must be questioning, self-examining, open, and involved.

- If children are to be nurturing, they must develop a social conscience.

- In order to maximize benefits of interdependence, hierarchy should be minimized; interdependence is a nonhierarchical relationship.

- Authority should be the accepted based upon nurture, wisdom, and judgment, empathy, not dominance.

- Moral growth is necessary, and repentance and apology facilitate and presuppose the possibility for moral growth.

Key words encapsulating values of Nurturant Parent morality are **empathy, nurturance, self-nurturance, social ties, fairness, and happiness.** Kathy is sitting on the average pew, in the average church, on the average Sunday in America.

Conservative and Liberal Demons

There is a perilous underside to each moral order. It is this treacherous underside that provides the impetus and justification to harm and do violence to people. People are demonized, and it becomes legitimate to suspend decency and discriminate against, despise, hate, hurt, maim, and in the worst instances even to kill in some perverted form of righteous indignation in the name of God or some high-minded ideal. Each moral order has a demonology and demonizes citizens of the other worldview. These demonic citizens, by the very nature of who they are, violate one of more of the conservative or progressive moral categories, and the more categories they violate, the more demonic they are. Most people will not admit that they are demonizing people; one strategy is to gain control of the voting and law-making machinery, and when laws are passed based in one's worldview, citizens can feign ignorance and naiveté. Many adherents will deem their hands clean of hate and demonology because the system does the work. Or, the other way demonology is framed is to shape difference as a cultural war, and therefore whatever one does to the other side is justified because in any war, demonization of the other side is necessary as a rationale to suspend normal moral actions and judgments and do what is necessary to win.

Lakoff lists an extensive demonology and inventories for both worldviews' Category 1 to Category 5 Demons. First, let's look at **demons for conservatives:**

CONSERVATIVE
DEMONS

The Unconscious Moral Worldview and the Dangerous Sermon

Category 1 Demons: anyone who by their very nature is against conservative values and Strict Father morality such as feminists, womanists, LGBTQI, and other "deviants" who are at the top of the list since by their very nature they oppose Strict Father morality. Others include advocates of multiculturalism, post-modern humanists who deny absolute values, and egalitarians who are against moral authority, moral order, and any other kind of hierarchy.

Category 2 Demons: those who lack self-discipline, which has led to a lack of self-reliance. Unwed mothers are high on the list, since their lack of sexual control has led to their dependence on the state. Others are unemployed drug users, whose drug habit has led to their being unable to support themselves, and able-bodied people on welfare, who can work but aren't working. In this land of opportunity they are assumed to be lazy and desire to be dependent on others.

Category 3 Demons: protectors of the "public good" such as environmentalists, consumer advocates, advocates of affirmative action, and advocates of government-supported universal health care; anyone who wants the government to interfere with the pursuit of self-interest and thus constrain business activities in the name of the common good.

Category 4 Demons: those who oppose the ways that the unbridled military and criminal justice systems have operated, including anti-war protesters, advocates of prisoners' rights, opponents of police brutality, gun-control advocates, Black Lives Matter activists, and so on. Abortion doctors may be the worst since they directly kill the most innocent people of all, the unborn.

Category 5 Demons: These are advocates of equal rights for women, gays, blacks, nonwhites, and ethnic Americans. They work to upset the moral order.

Without question, because she violates all five categories, the demon of demons has principally been Hillary Clinton, then Nancy Pelosi, and now Alexandria Ocasio-Cortez.

Second, by way of comparison and contrast, let's look at **demons for progressives**:

Category 1 Demons: the mean-spirited, selfish, and unfair; those who have no empathy and show no sense of social responsibility. Wealthy companies and businesspeople who only care about profit are at the top of the list, and get away with so much because of their money and power that buys political influence and the criminal justice system.

Category 2 Demons: those that would ignore, harm, or exploit the disadvantaged. Union-busting companies are a classic example, as are large agricultural firms that exploit farm workers, for example, by exposing them to poisonous pesticides and paying them poorly.

Category 3 Demons: those whose activities harm the social environment. They include violent criminals, out-of-control police, polluters, those who make unsafe products or engage in consumer fraud, developers with no sense of ecology, and large companies that make extensive profits from government subsidies (e.g., mining, brazing, water, and lumber subsidies) by contributing to the coffers of politicians.

Category 4 Demons: those who oppose public support of education, art, and scholarships—public welfare that leads to the common good.

Category 5 Demons: those against the expanse of health care for the general public and the seriousness of change to combat climate change.

Because he violates all five categories, the demon of all demons for progressives is Donald J. Trump, then Mitch McConnell, and Lindsay Graham.

Conservative and Liberal Christianity

Many liberal and progressive Christians have criticized the connection between conservative religion and conservative politics, with the most recent evidence of this symbiotic relationship in the fact that 80 percent of evangelicals supported and still vigorously support the candidacy and presidency of Donald J. Trump, who would seem to be at odds with conservative Christian belief and strict moral judgment of behaviors. From Lakoff's perspective, liberal Christianity connects liberal religion and liberal politics as well. There are many and various interpretations of Christianity, and it is difficult to fit them simply into the categories of liberal and conservative, though most models seem, for the sake of discussion, to reflect some form of liberal and conservative belief.

For Lakoff, there is no such thing as a neutral Christianity, and both conservative and liberal Christianity reflect the social values of the models of family on which they are based. He suggests the Bible does not argue one definitive interpretation or the other. Despite arguments to the contrary, and seeming to lean heavily on Strict Father morality, the Bible does not prefer one moral system or family model. Family models are imposed on the Bible based upon hermeneutics or cultural interpretations. Lakoff argues something similar to our argument about one's social location being an important factor in one's working gospel and theology in the previous chapter. The Bible, in and of itself, says nothing about the kind of politics one should have. Conservative Christianity is based upon the Strict Father family model and progressive Christianity on the Nurturant Parent interpretation of the Bible, and both lead to conservative or liberal religious politics, given, again, many variations and mixed views of Christianity. One's Christianity, and hence, one's politics, is based upon the passages that one pays the most attention to, or gives the most weight to, or the passages one gives less priority to, as I attempted to suggest in the previous chapter.

Lakoff is careful to suggest that the point is not "de-constructing" or making value judgements on conservative Christianity, or liberal Christianity for that matter. His point is that it is fundamentally human to choose a family model and then apply that family model to one's religion and politics. Family-based morality precedes morality based upon religion. Conservative Christians have a metaphorical interpretation of the Bible, and it happens to be Strict Father morality, and they apply that interpretation to their politics. Similarly, liberal Christians have a Nurturant Parent interpretation of the Bible, and they apply that interpretation to their politics as well. He argues this process is fundamentally human, corresponding with how the brain works according to cognitive science.

Dual Moral Orders and Preaching Dangerous Sermons

After all this detail, the reader is probably asking: Specifically, what does all of this cognitive theory have to do with preaching dangerous sermons? Let me remind the reader of the three assertions that we began this chapter with. First, preachers must understand their own moral worldview and how that worldview shapes and influences the theology and working gospel that sculpts their preaching, even their conservative or liberal Christianity. Lakoff's theory allows us to take an objective step back from our moral worldview and bring unconscious assumptions of our moral order to conscious thought for examination, analysis, and clarification, which presents the opportunity to be more receptive to a different and even opposing worldview. Objectivity allows emotional distance that helps cool our emotional jets and critically analyze our own moral order, including our theology, working gospel, dominance hierarchy, politics, and our Christianity itself. This level of objectivity helps us especially confront our fears, prejudices, stereotypes, racism, and any other negative emotions that would allow us to rationalize diminishment or even demonization of a person or an opposing worldview. This does not necessarily mean that we give up our worldview, but we think through more carefully and critically our assumptions and give ourselves the best chance to deliver ourselves from unconscious bias, division, polarization, and demonization in the American social, political, and religious landscape.

Second, if we understand and accept the reality of our own and different moral worldviews, we can better rhetorically shape the dangerous sermon in the manner that gives it the best chance to be heard. With more objective clarity about our own and the worldview and Christianity of others, we can more easily discern constructive and healing rhetorical patterns of argumentation and persuasion. We are able to understand with even more clarity Lakoff's insightful claim that "facts have to be framed in appropriately moral terms to be taken seriously." We might even be able to see places of agreement in an opposing worldview and Christianity, and therefore comprehend opportunities to bridge. In the next chapter, I will explore in greater detail a specific example of how a dangerous sermon might have better rhetorically shaped to facilitate an improved hearing.

Third, if preachers understood different moral orders and Christianity, they are in the best position to help a congregation understand moral orders that they might not agree with or be familiar with or normally would not associate with and even demonize. The preacher that would preach dangerous sermons must accept an educational and inspirational role. Based upon the preacher's knowledge of dual moral orders, the preacher educates the congregation to perspectives of the other moral order and Christianity.

This education can take the shape of presenting facts, data, and other information based in objective reality. The preacher must always remember that for an opposing audience this only speaks to 2 percent of the conscious thought of the brain. To reach an opposing worldview, information must always be coupled with inspiration to reach the 98 percent unconscious thought of the brain. The best of all faith traditions inspires hearers to relate to others they are not familiar with, avoid, or even demonize. Rhetorical strategies must have a combination of education and inspiration to reach the embedded unconscious. One of my major teachers and mentors, Henry H. Mitchell, drilled us over and over in classes that in preaching we must both "illumine and inspire."

In sum total, the preacher who is aware of different moral orders and Christianity has the ability to develop messages that invite people beyond accidental and unintentional divisive rhetoric and polarizations. The preacher has the moral dexterity and rhetorical agility to go well beyond glib religious and cultural usage of labels, stereotypes, tribal tropes, prejudices, divisive language, and especially demonization to speak to the heart of the faith tradition that brings people together by inspiring wonder, mystery, and hope rather than division and polarization.

I believe the immense challenge in preaching dangerous sermons is to navigate the unconscious worldview, religious belief systems, and cultural political views of hearers in order to say what needs to be said. In all likelihood, the preacher who preaches effective dangerous sermons is going to have to bridge into different worldviews or expand the worldview of the people who agree with the preacher. It is really fun, uplifting, and sometimes critically necessary to preach sermons to people of our worldview and reinforce the togetherness and assuredness of our morality. For preachers, it is a sugar high like no other—an audience that agrees, fawns, and feigns because all is right with the world because we are right. But sometimes we are called to challenge our own worldview and the worldview of those who agree with us. We have the responsibility to preach sermons that help both worldviews become more open, flexible, and inclusive to different perspectives. If we want an effective and dangerous sermon that educates, challenges, and inspires, whether the audience is progressive, moderate, or conservative, the theological and rhetorical arguments must be placed with the worldview of the audience.

Admittedly, the preaching task is daunting and almost impossible with these suggestions, and yet, many of us preach dangerous sermons anyway. The example of Jesus preaching to his home congregation in Luke 4 is an example and reminder that, despite our best efforts, sometimes it does not go particularly well. Is it so bad to have to demonstrate faith and the courage of our conviction, regardless of the consequences, every now and then? The biblical record is full of people who took just such a risk. Why would we assume that this might not be our calling as well? The question is: Can we sleep at night, preaching a gospel with no risk?

Bridging into My Moral Worldview

I am not suggesting herein that a preacher give up his or her worldview to engage an audience or person from an opposing worldview. One of the benefits of the exploration of Lakoff's cognitive theory of unconscious moral order has been the opportunity to examine my own moral worldview and Christianity. In comparing Lakoff's liberal worldview to the conservative worldview, I have had to question myself as to what I believe and why. I have had to bring unconscious beliefs to conscious light for critical examination. I have learned many things about both myself and liberal and conservative belief.

For the most part, I considered conservative thought a hodge-podge of issue-by-issue convenient positions based in partisan arguments cast to win elections and to defend political decisions and conservative positions at all costs. What I saw was a consistent personal and petty rage based in conspiracy theories, cultural wars, and victim ideology. What has become evident is presently an almost blind cult of personality with a lack of moral backbone or courage to stand up for stated conservative principles. In my research before writing *How to Preach a Dangerous Sermon*, I read more broadly into conservative writers and was surprised that I found some commonality. I found a respectable coherence in the conservative position, worldview, and Christianity. This conservative worldview, and the liberal worldview for that matter, is not well-represented by the political squabbles heard through the megaphone of cable news and social media. The focus tends to be day to day and issue-oriented rather than family-based moral conceptual systems and long-term systems. I have come to see the best of conservatism as ordinary people defending what they deeply believe is right. I have come to respect the broader principles of conservatism, even as I have lost respect for the petty politics and religious support I see for conservative politicians and the conservative party in its Trumpian iteration.

Because I understand the conservative position better does not mean that I agree. I hold to the argument that most conservatives never seem to include critical analyses of race, misogyny, patriarchy, immigration, discrimination, homophobia, capitalism, big business, and wealth inequality. While I believe that hierarchy is, at some level, necessary in life, the function of hierarchy is service to the common good and not dominance.

I find it extremely difficult to accept this aforementioned conservative dominance hierarchy:

> Human beings over Nature; Adults over Children; the Rich over the Poor (and hence, Employers over Employees); Western Culture over Non-Western Culture; Our Country over Other Countries…Men over Women; Whites over Nonwhites; Straights over Gays; Christians over Non-Christians.[9]

White supremacists, when they get in power, implement this conservative dominance hierarchy and create systems, influence structures, and pass laws that ensure systems, structures, and institutions reflect their racial, sexual, and gender identity and therefore their bias.

As an African American person, why would I accept the pre-ordained dominance of whites? Why would I accept a second-class status along with a wide section of the population? How can you see me as an equal, if you believe that you are higher on the socially constructed dominance hierarchy and claim objective reality and divine right? This dominance hierarchy is tinged with self-interest and sin. This dominance hierarchy is historically and presently stained with the legacy of slavery, racism, lynching, sexual violence, abuse of women, demeaning violence against the LGBTQI community, mass incarceration, discrimination from xeno-phobia, homophobia, patriarchy, and narcissism. First Americans were virtually exterminated and their land stolen from them. There has been, and is now, a huge struggle in this country to overcome the domination and power narrative of white supremacy. I fight white supremacy with every fiber of my being.

We have spent time talking about the speaker bridging into the world-view of an audience. Let's ask what would it take for the conservative worldview to bridge into my mostly progressive worldview.

There are some parts of the conservative worldview that I agree with and that make sense to me, such as hard work, self-discipline, and self-reliance as key ethical values without which it is impossible to be success-ful in life. I believe in these values and have tried to demonstrate them in my life. This is an area at which a conservative speaker might bridge

---

9. Lakoff, *Moral Politics*, 413.

into my moral worldview to make arguments that appeal to me. I can also agree that it is true that some are lazy, game the system, or need to say no to sex or drugs and that failure can be due to moral weakness. But I cannot agree with the demonization of whole groups of people as lazy and immoral without any understanding of individual circumstances and situations.

Poverty, for example, is based upon a myriad of factors, and I absolutely refuse to accept that society has no role to play in and no responsibility for poverty. Poverty is not singularly an issue of individual morals. To bridge into my worldview, the speaker would have to admit that public resources flow to some communities, and as a result, those communities have quality housing, health-care services, schools, and grocery stores. They have economic development, effective policing, and the concern of politicians. As I said, following Patrick Sharkey, in *How to Preach a Dangerous Sermon*:

> Suburban prosperity, where it exists, has been facilitated by federal investment in a highway and regional transportation systems that allowed firms and workers to relocate outside of the central city. The expansion of home ownership in suburban American was possible because of federally backed mortgages, and home owners continue to be the recipients of the largest housing policy the federal government operates: the home mortgage interest deduction, which disproportionately benefits middle- and upper-income homeowners and dwarfs any housing policy targeting low-income populations.[10]

I might be open to the conservative worldview if there could be a discussion that one factor in poverty and wealth is that some have access to public resources and others do not. I cannot accept the personal-responsibility argument alone. I can accept some personal responsibility, but I refuse to let society off the hook in its role of who has poverty and who has wealth.

I can also agree that there is abuse of the welfare system. If a conservative moral worldview speaker highlighted the double standard in regards to welfare in America, I could be persuaded. I cannot accept the demonization of unwed mothers, particularly black mothers, and the elevation

---

10. Frank A. Thomas, *How to Preach a Dangerous Sermon* (Nashville: Abingdon Press, 2018), 1, 8–9.

and sainthood bestowed on corporations and the ultra-rich, who receive welfare and government largesse as well. For example, Lakoff points out that after the 1994 elections, Secretary of Labor Robert Reich sought to challenge conservative model citizens and large successful corporations and those who run them. Reich pointed out that conservatives demonized welfare recipients but did not attack corporations and the ultra-rich for "corporate welfare." Large corporations and the ultra-rich were the beneficiaries of large amounts of government welfare that they did not earn, including:

> money from inordinately cheap grazing rights, mineral and timber rights, infrastructure development that supports their businesses, agricultural price supports, and hundreds of other kinds of enormous government largesse that come out of tax payer's pocketbook—an amount far exceeding the cost of social programs. If the government eliminated corporate welfare, Reich argued, then it could easily afford social programs to help the poor.[11]

Reich's attempt to critique conservative model citizens failed summarily. The saintly status of successful corporations and the ultra-rich, and hence capitalism itself, is almost beyond critique in America, as if the brains of capitalists and free market adherents automatically delete any critique or restrictions on capitalism. The moment one critiques capitalism, even crony capitalism, or patrimonial capitalism, one is quickly labeled as a socialist. I might be able to accept the critique of welfare recipients by the conservative worldview if they would make the critique equal across the board. Critique all welfare corporate, rich, middle-class, and poor with the same brush and do not single out and demonize the poor for critique and laud the rich as innovative and as wealth creators. If the conservative moral worldview had an equal critique, I might be open to meaningful conversation about welfare reform.

Of course, these kinds of discussions require nuance, equanimity, patience, deliberation, multiple conversations, and patient dialogue. These are the kinds of discussions that, by bridging moral worldviews across time, make moral progress. The tendency from within our worldview is

---

11. Thomas, *How to Preach a Dangerous Sermon,* 172.

to skip conversation and dialogue and go right to outrage, such as "tear down the statue" or "lock her up." This is not to say that some forms of oppression and violence warrant outrage and immediate relief, but it is wise to remember that ultimate truth is always the domain of nuance and discussion and is connected to understanding and bridging the worldview of others. Our moral worldview can win elections with taunts, threats, negative language, nativism, racism, cheating, and so on, but sadly and far too soon, we will discover the consequences of not having made any moral progress: democracy will perish from the face of the earth. What's at stake in this discussion of dueling moral imaginations is whether our democracy will survive.

In all candor and truth, I cannot be certain that Lakoff's theory of bridging into the worldview of others works the majority of the time. We are dealing with the embedded unconscious emotions and beliefs that have been hard-wired into human consciousness—some, I would argue, for generations. I remember a time when I was in extended counseling sessions and learning the family systems theory that would help me change my life. The coach would say this to me at the end of most sessions: "Family systems theory always works until you apply it to your own family." In other words, many theories work in the learning and discussion phase, but it is a different matter when you apply it to the real world of embedded and unconscious emotions operative in most of the human family. My coach would say as the final word to encourage me, "God bless you and do the best you can." Theory in the abstract works; it is in the application of theory in the rough-and-tumble world of human reality and interactions that every theory gets put to the test. God bless us all and may we all do our very best.

In the next chapter, I would like to take a look at the eulogy delivered by Rev. Jasper Williams Jr. at the funeral celebration of Aretha Franklin. It was a dangerous sermon, and I want to look at the clash of moral worldviews and working theologies in the responses to the sermon. I want to explore, through a tangible example, how we might bridge into another moral worldview.

Chapter Four

"SOMETHING MUST BE DONE": A RHETORICAL READING OF REV. JASPER WILLIAMS JR.'S EULOGY OF ARETHA FRANKLIN

[Rev. Jasper Williams] delivered a very conservative sermon, akin to spanking your kids in public, an act which many might find out of date and abusive, but which others might celebrate as necessary to a goal of restoring discipline and respect.... And let my mother tell it, he was right on point, but my academic friend folk think he needs to be tarred and feathered.

—John Sims and Alisea Williams McLeod

On August 16, 2018, the Queen of Soul, Aretha Franklin, died following a battle with cancer at her home in Detroit, Michigan. The news of her death spread far, fast, and wide in newsprint, television, cable news, and social media, triggering a massive outpouring of condolences, well-wishes, grief, tears, and prayers from around the world and all over America, and especially so in her hometown of Detroit. Her music was played in continuous loops across the airwaves as indisputable evidence to

65

the tremendous number of lives that she touched both in her music and in her social activism.

There was immediate public interest in saying "good-bye" to Aretha Franklin in a funeral celebration of her life. Eventually, the date and venue were established as August 31 and the four-thousand-seat Greater Grace Temple in Detroit, Michigan. Rev. Jasper Williams Jr., a powerful preacher and pastor emeritus of Salem Bible Church in Atlanta, Georgia, was chosen to deliver the eulogy. On August 23, a special news conference was held by Williams. Vast throngs of people made their way to Detroit for the celebration, and millions more watched nationally and globally on television and the internet.

After almost seven hours of the celebrative service, with various celebrities, entertainers, preachers, and personalities performing, singing, and making remarks, comments, and speeches, Williams rose to deliver the eulogy. Williams preached a dangerous sermon. Remember, we defined a dangerous sermon as a sermon, based in the preacher's moral imagination, that upends and challenges the dominant moral hierarchy that operates in the church and/or cultural context of the preaching event. I am confining the majority of my analysis and discussion to the black community because Williams's eulogy intentionally and directly addressed the black community. The eulogy was generally intended for anyone who wanted to celebrate the life of Aretha Franklin, and specifically it was a prophetic call aimed and targeted to challenge the black community to change direction and create R-E-S-P-E-C-T.

Within the black community, the eulogy was immediately and strongly condemned and also intensely supported and celebrated. Passionate discussion ensued, and in the upcoming pages, I would like to explore the eulogy from the perspective of the eulogist, the black community, the media, and the Franklin family. Williams's eulogy highlighted longstanding differences and difficult discussions circulating for generations in the black community concerning how to spiritually, strategically, and effectively deal with white supremacy and racism in America. John Simms and Alisea Williams McLeod capture the big-picture impact of the funeral service to black America:

It also was a family reunion with all of the drama and inappropriateness that come with diversity and intergenerationality, and different degrees of pain. This event tried to straddle both the public and private language and behavior of Black church culture around its most sacred performance—the death ritual....So it was only a matter of time before something was going to pop off...where the club look meets the church vibe, where gospel meets R&B, where the male gaze meets female bodies, and youthful body expression meets the restraint of religious respectability.[1]

My goal herein is to have a substantive discussion of the eulogy based upon what I have stated in the last two chapters in reference to Resner's concept of working gospel and Lakoff's understanding of dual worldviews and moral orders. The method of analysis that I will utilize is a form of rhetorical criticism. Rhetorical criticism is the study of the various persuasive options available to speakers in the creation of speech texts (in this instance a eulogy) and how those options work together to create effects in the preacher and audience. Rhetorical criticism allows us to see with greater clarity the persuasive choices the preacher made, potentially to see other choices that were not selected, and in this case, for the sake of analysis, to suggest rhetorical choices for the preacher that might have made the sermon more persuasive, especially to those who disagreed.

Of course, I am being presumptive and mean no disrespect to Rev. Jasper Williams Jr. This eulogy is a great sermon to analyze how one preaches a dangerous sermon and unintentionally generates such controversy. This eulogy allows us to make guesses at rhetorical choices the preacher could have made, or any preacher can make when faced with a dangerous sermon, in order to be intentionally inclusive as possible in preaching.

This eulogy is also an unusual rhetorical artifact because rarely do we have the eulogist call a press conference, preach the eulogy, and call another press conference after the eulogy to respond to critics and supporters. This eulogy presents us with a prime opportunity to ascertain if in fact the thesis of this book holds any water, if preachers would be helped in examining their working gospel, moral worldview and order, and the dominance hierarchies embedded therein, and those of their audience,

1. John Sims and Alisea Williams McLeod, "Aretha Franklin: A Detroit Conversation," September 11, 2018, https://medium.com/@timetraveler3/aretha-franklin-funering-a-queen-f78aba715d6d.

such that the sermon has the best chance to be heard by the broadest number of people possible. Ultimately, my hope is that the preacher who is aware of different moral orders and working gospels has the ability to develop messages that invite people beyond accidental and unintentional divisive rhetoric and polarizations by speaking to the heart of the inclusive faith tradition that brings people together by inspiring wonder, mystery, and hope.

I want to briefly look at the working gospel and the unconscious moral order of Williams and propose that the working gospel and moral order of his critics might be different than his. As a matter of fact, criticism and support might cluster around the same or different working gospel and/or the same Strict Father or Nurturant Parent morality. Based upon this analysis, I will offer reflections of how Williams, had he recognized different working gospels and different moral orders, might have bridged into the other worldview, such that his arguments might have been persuasive.

It is important to begin discussion by looking closely at the Williams press conference before the eulogy, the eulogy itself as delivered, the responses to the eulogy, including that of the Franklin family, and the press conference after the eulogy, and finally I will discern intentional alternative rhetorical strategies that might have given the eulogy a broader appeal.

The Press Conference Announcing the Eulogist[2]

Our critical examination of the eulogy begins with an August 23, 2018, press conference held by Rev. Jasper Williams Jr. Williams introduced himself, announced that he was the eulogist for the funeral of Aretha Franklin, and then answered questions from the media. The length of the press conference was 16:47 and subsequently addressed three main points of information in response to questions asked of Williams by the media: (1) the relationship of Aretha Franklin and Williams such as to

---

2. "Aretha Franklin Eulogy to Be Delivered by Rev. Jasper Williams, Jr.," press conference, YouTube video, August 23, 2018, https://www.youtube.com/watch?time_continue=10&v=1Vm7djjtNug.

understand how Williams was selected to do the eulogy; (2) how Williams was preparing for the eulogy and what message he was preparing to give; and (3) the challenge of delivering the eulogy and Williams's request for prayer in shaping a eulogy that would meet expectations.

In the effort to explain how he was selected for the eulogy, Williams commented that his parents were from the state of Mississippi and so were the parents of Aretha Franklin. Williams explained that Aretha's father, Rev. C. L. Franklin, lived side by side on Lucy Street in Memphis, Tennessee, with his uncle, Rev. A. R. Williams (Uncle Buddy).[3] They played checkers together, and a friendship developed between them. Because of this "heritage of our parenthood," he crossed paths with Aretha Franklin when he was sixteen or seventeen years old.

Williams further illustrated his connection to the family by stating that he preached the eulogy of Aretha Franklin's father, Rev. C. L. Franklin, on August 11, 1984. Aretha's father was shot in 1979 and stayed in a coma for five years. He described the details of how Aretha asked him to do her father's funeral and how he considered it "providential" that he was asked by her again almost thirty-four years later in the same month of August. Because of his relationship with family, he was selected to do the eulogy.

When asked by the media what inspired him the most about Aretha Franklin's legacy, Williams emphatically responded, "That's Rev. Franklin's daughter. Rev. Franklin was the icon, guru preacher of my whole life. He mentored me." One critical prism through which Williams saw the eulogy was the legacy, presence, and impact of his relationship with Aretha's father, Rev. C. L. Franklin.

When asked by a reporter, in essence, who Jasper Williams is and what his legacy is, Williams remarked that he saw himself as being the recipient of the mantle of Franklin. He mentions the biblical story of Elijah the prophet, who had a young understudy named Elisha (2 Kings 2). Elisha wanted the anointing of Elijah on his life. Elijah said that if Elisha saw him when was taken from him, he would receive the anointing, otherwise he

---

3. Reverend C. L. (Clarence LaVaughn) Franklin (1915–84), pulpiteer and preacher extraordinaire, helped take the tradition of black preaching to new heights as he whooped his often-extemporaneous sermons. Franklin was the most popular preacher of his generation and likely the most imitated African American preacher in history.

would not. Elijah was caught up on a chariot and taken in a whirlwind to heaven. Elisha saw it, picked up Elijah's cloak, and did the same miracle as Elijah, signifying that the anointing of Elijah has passed on to Elisha. Williams says:

> That is the way that I perceive and think of myself as it relates to the late Dr. C. L. Franklin. He was the prophet, the guru, the greatest preacher of the 20th century. When I was privileged to preach his funeral, I internalized that as being the recipient of the mantle that he had. The same anointing and the same mantle that had blessed and anointed his ministry somehow fell on me. I am humbled, pleased and proud.[4]

In addition, when asked how he was going to prepare, Williams responded that he would take the life of Aretha and the word of God, look at society as it is in the present, and bring it all together. When asked in a follow-up question about insights into what he would be saying, Williams asked for prayer and said that he was trying to come up with the right approach. He wanted to represent himself, his church, and the city of Atlanta.

When asked, "What do you want people to know about Aretha Franklin after everything has been said after this funeral?" Williams commented:

> I want everybody to know Aretha will be eternalized in all of our minds and hearts and she should be eternalized because in some shape form or fashion she touched all of us. The only reason that we have concern about Aretha Franklin now is because of what she did in her songs that reached all of us. So from soul to soul, I see this: I am a spirit; I have a soul, and I live in my body, the trichotomy of mankind and I see that expressed in the life and legacy Aretha lived and what she tried to do.[5]

Williams was asked to speak about Aretha Franklin's significance to the black church based upon the fact that she was a soul singer and a great gospel singer. Williams reflectively said, "She is the Queen of Soul."[6] Williams defined soul music as gospel, jazz, pop, and rock all meshed into a

---

4. "Aretha Franklin Eulogy to Be Delivered by Rev. Jasper Williams, Jr."
5. "Aretha Franklin Eulogy to Be Delivered by Rev. Jasper Williams, Jr."
6. "Aretha Franklin Eulogy to Be Delivered by Rev. Jasper Williams, Jr."

rhythm of blues that provides soul music. Because of all that being one, Williams believed that "God must be in it somewhere."[7]

Finally, when asked what people could do to participate, Williams asked everyone to remember him in prayer. One of the overarching themes of the press conference was Williams asking for support in prayer from everyone. Williams explained that this task was difficult because Aretha Franklin was an icon with many different aspects, and he felt insignificant to do the eulogy. He said: "But with God, with my church praying and even you who are watching—including watchers and cameramen—if all of us pray, the Lord will meet us there."[8] Reporters were surprised, based upon the fact that Williams was a legend in black preaching and had great tenure in age and ministry (seventy-five years of age, preaching for sixty-eight years, and pastoring a church for fifty-five years), that he would have difficulty or be challenged. Williams asserts, maybe for all preachers: "One thing I have learned—never be certain and assured of yourself in a pulpit when it comes to doing anything for God. You ask me if I am struggling. I will be struggling until I am finished preaching that funeral—that is the way it is with me."[9]

A Close Reading of "Aretha: The Queen of Soul"

After a close reading of Williams's eulogy entitled "Aretha: The Queen of Soul," I am presenting my summary in a fair amount of detail because frequently excerpts and comments from sermons, speeches, and interviews are taken out of context, and positions of support or criticism are forged without a reading of the entire statement or without seeking to understand the overall environment. We live in a soundbite age, when many opinions are formed on social media or cable news, and in far too many cases, meanings are distorted without an appeal to the broader

---

7. "Aretha Franklin Eulogy to Be Delivered by Rev. Jasper Williams, Jr."
8. "Aretha Franklin Eulogy to Be Delivered by Rev. Jasper Williams, Jr."
9. "Aretha Franklin Eulogy to Be Delivered by Rev. Jasper Williams, Jr."

context. Context matters and whether one is in support of or in criticism of a particular position, it is a matter of justice and fairness to read and understand the broader perspective. This is some of the reason that I started with the Williams press conference to announce the eulogy and will end with the Williams press conference after the eulogy responding to supporters and critics. It is important that we rightly judge by understanding what was actually said and by giving as much of the context as possible.

The eulogy has five movements, "Opening Hymn and Subject," "God Crowned Aretha Franklin the Queen of Soul," "Challenge to the Black Community to Regain Its Soul," "Rev. C. L. Franklin's Love for His Daughter," and closing "Celebration and R-E-S-P-E-C-T." In the movement including celebration, Williams begins to whoop. I will spend a brief amount of time helping the reader unfamiliar with whooping to understand its importance and significance as an art form.

Movement One: Opening Hymn and Subject

Williams opens the eulogy by mentioning that thirty-four years ago he eulogized Aretha's father. From the very outset, Williams brings the memory and legacy of Rev. C. L. Franklin front and center. We discussed much of this in the aforementioned press conference section, but the context of the eulogy is the mentor role that Franklin played in the life of Williams. Williams has adopted the mantle of Franklin and lifts the very prayer hymn that Franklin opened with each time he preached, the Charles Wesley hymn "Father I Stretch My Hands to Thee."[10]

Williams sings the first verse and invites Dottie Peoples, affectionately called the "Songbird of the South," to lead both him and the congregation in the repeat verse of the song. Based upon Franklin's practice, the song has become somewhat of a standard for a generation of African American Baptist preachers. Large parts of the African American audience were already familiar with the hymn, and most could easily sing it without written words. Following the song, Williams announces his subject: "Aretha:

---

10. Lyrics to this hymn can be found online at https://www.lyriczz.com/lyrics/charles-wesley/45307-father,-i-stretch-my-hands-to-thee/.

The Queen of Soul." In most African American preaching, a preacher tries to sum up the entire message with a title that seeks to arrest the attention of the audience. With the prayer hymn sung and the subject announced Williams concludes the first movement of the eulogy.

Movement Two: God Crowned Aretha Franklin the Queen of Soul

William begins the second move by informing the audience that in May 1964, at the Chicago Regal Theatre, a local disc jockey, Spann Cooper (actually Pervis Spann), anointed and crowned Aretha Franklin as the Queen of Soul. Williams elevates her crowning to the eternal level by stating that God crowned her Queen of Soul long before Cooper. This leads Williams to his biblical text, Genesis 2:7 (KJV), which reads, "The Lord God formed man of the dust of the ground, and breathed into his nostrils the breath of life; and man became a living soul." He begins to teach by mentioning the trichotomy that he discussed in the press conference. The dust of the ground is the body (soma), the breath of the body is the spirit (pneuma), and the soul is the inner man, his emotions and will (psyche). God breathed and man became a living soul. God formed man like a potter takes clay and shapes it to form a vessel. God was totally involved in the fashioning of mankind. Williams concludes his theology of the soul by having the congregation to repeat after him: "I am a spirit; I have a soul; I live in my body."[11]

Williams returns to Aretha Franklin and asks how the (title of) Queen of Soul connects with God. The title itself comes from black culture. It alludes to a form of music, known as soul music. What is soul music? Soul music is the combination of gospel, jazz, rock, and pop that gets meshed into an urban rhythm kind of blues. All of the various musics are wrapped up in soul music, and as a result, for Williams, there must be a God somewhere.

Williams asks what this word *soul* means. What is soul? Metaphorically, he brings Rev. C. L. Franklin to the stage to define soul based upon Franklin's 1955 album, *The 23rd Psalm*. In verse three of Psalm 23, the biblical

11. "Aretha Franklin Eulogy."

text says, "He restoreth my soul," and Rev. Franklin takes the opportunity to define soul: "Nobody can really say what soul is. As close as we can come to defining soul is to say that soul is that part of man that is a little bit like God."[12] Williams concludes, "This means God in man is soul."[13]

William then raises the major complication of the sermon that he seeks to resolve: human beings have lost their souls. He tells a story of a slave put in charge of a child for his master for several months. The master returns several months later and the slave saved his clothes but lost the child. Williams draws the parallel that one day he would stand before God and say that we cherished our body, that we bathed and washed it and took all kind of extravagant care of it, but then would report that we lost our soul. He remarks, "How cold, chilling, and non-redeeming to say Master, Sir, I lost my soul."[14] He asks the audience to check the condition of their soul: "The part of us that is supposed to be like God, have you lost your soul? Have you lost your relationship with God?"[15] Williams sums up the matter by asserting that one hundred years from now, the only thing that will matter is if your soul has been saved. The second move of the sermon has been completed.

Movement Three: Challenge to the Black Community to Regain Its Soul

Williams asks the audience to shift and pay attention to the fact that the eyes of the world are upon this home-going celebration. He asks how they can take the iconic stature of Aretha Franklin and say Aretha's life and legacy brought real true change to the world. As she is carried to her resting place, Williams's goal is to immortalize the Queen of Soul.

He shifts to directly address the black community and challenges the African American community "to remove the veneer, lay aside the prejudice, set aside the bias, and take a good clean look at where we are in black

12. "Aretha Franklin Eulogy."
13. "Aretha Franklin Eulogy."
14. "Aretha Franklin Eulogy."
15. "Aretha Franklin Eulogy."

America."[16] If black America is truthful, honest, and fair, then it must say that it has lost its soul and that it must come back home to God. He slips into a poetic refrain: "Hush—listen, I hear the queen echoing in the wind—something must be done, done, done! Something must be done, done, done! Something must be done, done, done! The queen is wanting to issue a mandate—sign her executive order—*something must be done, done, done!*"[17]

He mentions Aretha's support of the civil rights movement and how she worked for Martin Luther King Jr. and took no money. She sang "Precious Lord" at Dr. King's funeral in 1968. Aretha spoke up and delivered Angela Davis out of jail. Her father objected because of the fear of being called a communist, but Aretha said, "She is a black woman and had no one to help her and I wanted to help her. Period."[18] He returns to his refrain: *So I hear her voice again, rumbling through the echo of the wind— something must be done, done, done—something must be done, done, done!*

He reminds the audience that the black race once had a thriving economy. The black race had its own hotels, grocery stores, and banks, even as bad as the days of Jim Crow were. He takes the position that one good thing out of segregation was that it forced black people *to* each other rather than *on* each other. Black people came to quickly realize that all they had as a people was one another. He then issues a critique of the benefits of civil rights and integration: "But when we marched, when we protested, when we got through saying we shall overcome, yes we were rewarded with integration, we got what we fought for, we got what we marched for. But with the birth of integration, there also came the loss of not only the black community's economy, but there also came the loss of the black man's soul."[19]

Next, he addresses the concern of leadership in the home by suggesting that as he looks into the houses of black men, there are no fathers in the home: "Seventy per cent of our households are led by our precious, proud, fine black women. But as beautiful and fine as our black women

---

16. "Aretha Franklin Eulogy."
17. "Aretha Franklin Eulogy."
18. "Aretha Franklin Eulogy."
19. "Aretha Franklin Eulogy."

are, one thing a black woman cannot do. A black woman cannot raise a black boy to be a man. She can't do that. She can't do that."[20]

The third concern is that black people are killing black people. He mentions a study released by Tuskegee in which the Ku Klux Klan killed 3,446 black people over an eighty-six-year span of time. Black people killed that number of people every six months. He does the math and suggests that black people kill 6,000-plus black people every year, and over an eighty-six-year span, 592,712 black people were killed by black people. He then says:

> It amazes me how it is that when the police kill one of us, we're ready to pro-test, march, destroy innocent property. We are ready to loot, steal, whatever we want....But when we kill one hundred of us nobody says anything. No-body does anything. Black on black crime, we're all doing time, we're locked up in our mind, there's got to be a better way, we must stop this today....If you choose to ask me today—Do black lives matter?...No. Black lives do not matter, black lives will not matter, black lives ought not matter, black lives should not matter, black lives must not matter until black people start respecting black lives and stop killing ourselves, black lives can never matter.[21]

He mentions that it hurts his heart to walk around black communities based upon people walking around like zombies, high, drunk, and on crack. These people are dismissed just as we dismiss flies. He asks as a refrain: "Where is your soul? Where is your God?" The third movement is now completed.

Movement Four: Rev. C. L. Franklin's Love for His Daughter

Williams asks the audience to "shift" and returns to the Queen's legacy: "What can we leave here saying that the queen of soul has done, is doing, or will do that will impact us as a race to turn our race around?"[22] He in-troduces Rev. Franklin into the discussion again by saying: "The eyes of the world are upon us today because of the late Dr. C. L. Franklin."[23] He then

---

20. "Aretha Franklin Eulogy."

21. "Aretha Franklin Eulogy."

22. "Aretha Franklin Eulogy."

23. "Aretha Franklin Eulogy."

talks about Franklin's marriage faltering and Franklin having to raise four children by himself. He does not intend to give the impression that Franklin exercised the best parenting skills. Based upon his awesome responsibility to preach the gospel and pastor his church, there was no way that he could adequately raise four children. Something in the home had to be wrong. There had to be a deficit somewhere because of the way that the Queen sang: "Most of the songs we heard her sing, particularly in her early years, we could feel the pain, feel the hurt, feel her backsets and setbacks in life, feel her heartaches and heartbreaks in life because they met our heartaches, backsets and setbacks. We could feel that when she sang her song: 'Natural Woman' and 'Ain't No Way,' all of those songs that she sang."[24] Williams is not saying anything negative about Franklin, because he comments that he went down the same road. His life has not been squeaky clean when it comes to home and the responsibility of his children. He comments that when parents fuss, argue, separate, and divorce, they are often not cognizant of the scars put upon children that they will never see until those children are out on their own. They see the scars upon their lives.

Franklin did the best that he could with parenting skills. Williams comments that it is difficult when we stray away from God's design for the home: "a man and a woman, a father and a mother, husband and a wife, a provider and a nurturer."[25] It is the man's responsibility to provide, and it is a woman's responsibility to nurture, that is, to give the child love and affection. Whenever a man is not there and provision is not made for the home, and whenever a mother is not there, and the child does not learn how to nurture and be loved and thereby learn to love, havoc will be the result. He says, "When the home is not like it ought to be, the father not doing his part and the mother not doing hers, the child has a deficit, abortion after birth."[26]

Williams argues that as a race, black people do not need better houses that government, big business, and big corporations can provide. Black people want to be given too much too often. Black people do not need better houses given to them, but they need to make better homes for

---

24. "Aretha Franklin Eulogy."

25. "Aretha Franklin Eulogy."

26. "Aretha Franklin Eulogy."

themselves. Black people need better homes. He then offers a metaphor-laden litany of differences between a house and a home. His main point is "a house is structural and a home is spiritual; a house is man's master design and a home is God's divine design."[27]

He returns to Franklin's parenting of Aretha and mentions that he did not limit his daughter's future based upon what he saw, or what he thought. Sometimes parents mess up their children when we try to force them to be what parents want them to be. It's the parents' responsibility to bring our children where God wants them to be. Williams states: "Dr. Franklin did a super-fantastic job that in making sure this his daughter had the kind of life [she wanted], in terms of her career."[28]

He then closes this fourth move with a story that reinforces Franklin's support of Aretha and her career. He recounts that Franklin was heavily criticized for the fact that he was a preacher of the gospel and his daughter sang the blues. He recounts a 1960 experience in Memphis, Tennessee, at Ellis Auditorium. The promoters promoted that Franklin would preach his famous sermon, "The Eagle Stirreth Her Nest," at 8:00 p.m., and at 10:00 p.m. Aretha Franklin would sing the blues. Many people went negative on Rev. Franklin because he was preaching the gospel and his daughter was singing the blues.

After preaching the sermon, Franklin sat down to listen to his daughter sing. There was confusion and controversy between those leaving after Franklin's sermon and those coming to hear Aretha sing the blues. Williams recounts, when Franklin sensed how confusing it was, he went to the microphone and said, "I wonder why you would treat me this way....Aretha is my daughter. I am getting ready to sit down on this stage and listen to my daughter sing the blues."[29] Williams recounts that he then said to his daughter, "Aretha, come on out here baby and sing the blues to your daddy."[30] Williams remembers that everybody in that place sat down, and the crowd who "shouted" (emotionally happy) when Franklin preached

27. "Aretha Franklin Eulogy."
28. "Aretha Franklin Eulogy."
29. "Aretha Franklin Eulogy."
30. "Aretha Franklin Eulogy."

"The Eagle Stirred Her Nest" was the same crowd who shouted when Aretha sang "Ain't No Way"—"that was his love for his daughter."[31] This closes the fourth movement, and Williams rides the emotion of the story of Franklin's daughter and begins to shift gears to whooping by adding music to his voice.

Movement Five: Celebration and R-E-S-P-E-C-T

One of the styles of the close or the celebration of the African American sermon is known as "whooping," and sometimes it is referred to as chanting, tuning, moaning, or intoning. The celebrative close of the sermon is very important in the black church and it is not just an emotional movement. The function of the celebration in the African American preaching tradition is to joyfully reinforce what the preacher has already taught the people. The preacher teaches and reinforces the teaching with joyful emotion. Martha Simmons, in an article entitled "Whooping: The Musicality of African American Preaching Past and Present," suggests that whooping can be thought of as a parallel to great opera: "The hearer is more readily caught up in the sermon, as one might be caught up in the dramatic power of an opera, because of the combined impact of tone and word."[32] Whooping then, is a form of proclamation (at the end of the sermon) "that transforms declarative and didactic speech into dramatic and celebratory song."[33] Simmons labels Franklin as having a "melodious, smooth whoop," and Williams, like many, followed the melodious whooping style of Franklin.[34]

---

31. "Aretha Franklin Eulogy."

32. Martha Simmons, "Whooping: The Musicality of African American Preaching Past and Present," in *Preaching with Sacred Fire: An Anthology of African American Sermons 1750–Present* (New York: W. W. Norton & Company, 2010), 865.

33. Simmons, "Whooping," 865.

34. Simmons, "Whooping," 873. Simmons says, "The ultimate melodious whooper was C. L. Franklin...[who] stands as the best known whooper of the twentieth century, as well as one of the most imitated. Many young whoopers from the 1950's to the 70's wanted to whoop like Frank (Franklin affectionately called Frank by many)." Simmons goes further to say, "not only could he whoop, his sermons were interesting, substantive, theologically strong, and relevant and he was a master at using metaphors. From 1965 to 1985, Franklin offered whooping classes, and preachers from across the country filled them."

As Williams changes gears from didactic speech to whooping, he makes a clear and direct call to action. In order to turn African American houses into homes, he calls for pastors across denominational, racial, and religious lines to lock arms together. For those who did not know where to go and what to do, he suggests starting in the neighborhoods around their churches and helping "struggling single moms that don't know what to do."[35] These single moms "need a man in the house through mentoring programs," and through "parenting our children, we can turn black America around."[36] He quotes the earlier refrain from the Queen: "Something must be done; something must be done!"[37] If the audience would hush and listen carefully, they could hear the voice of Aretha Franklin say that it is time black people change their direction around and come back home to God. Williams is now in full whoop.

In following a long line of black whoopers, he closes with poetry, hymnology, rhythm, cadence, repetition, and the melodious juxtaposition of words and music for unapologetic, powerful, and dramatic effect. Through whooping, he reinforces the points that he has already made in the eulogy: black America has lost its soul. Black America "has wandered far away from God, but now it is time to come home."[38] He quotes the Negro Spiritual "Ride on King Jesus," a well-known refrain in the black church that Jesus is the conquering King and that no one will hinder him, and therefore, he will overcome all manner of sin and evil.[39] He calls it a shame that we have allowed our children to be so wild that nobody—not the teacher, the pastor, or the police—can do anything with them: "It is time to turn Black America around."[40] He suggests that trouble in the world is based upon the trouble in the home: "The way the home goes is the way the world goes."[41] Ride on King Jesus. He quotes the popular

---

35. "Aretha Franklin's Eulogy."

36. "Aretha Franklin's Eulogy."

37. "Aretha Franklin's Eulogy."

38. "Aretha Franklin's Eulogy."

39. John Work, "Ride on King Jesus," Negro Spiritual, 1940, https://www.negrospirituals.com/songs/ride_on_king_jesus.htm.

40. "Aretha Franklin's Eulogy."

41. "Aretha Franklin's Eulogy."

and familiar lyrics: "What the world needs now is love sweet love."[42] He disputes that assertion by suggesting that it is "so hard to love somebody when you know they hate you. Aretha Franklin, the Queen of Soul told us all that we need to have a little R-E-S-P-E-C-T."[43] Williams makes an appeal for R-E-S-P-E-C-T rather than love by suggesting that "Democrats need to respect Republicans and Republicans need to respect Democrats; Liberals need to respect Conservatives and Conservatives need to respect Liberals, and he gives several more examples of groups needing to respect each other."[44] After the litany of everyone respecting everyone, he says, "The Queen did what she could and it is time for us to do what we can."[45] He then closes the eulogy with the lyrics from a well-known hymn in the traditional black church, "If when you give of the best of your service— God will! God will!—God will!"[46] Because the audience was familiar with the song, Williams only recited the first line, and the audience would have understood the rest, "Be not dismayed when men don't believe you. He'll understand and say, 'Well done.'" The implication is that God will understand and say, "Well done!" Williams closes the eulogy and then goes to his seat.

Public Reaction to the Eulogy

were these white critics?

Almost instantly, criticism of the eulogy went viral. Williams was accused of misogyny, bigotry, homophobia, perpetration of false science on race, demeaning black people, being "uneducated," parroting what Trump would say about the black community, and not honoring God, to mention a few. Several suggested that Williams's "plantation-style speech" is a prime example of the disconnect between young people and the older

---

42. "What the World Needs Now Is Love" is a popular 1965 song with lyrics by Hal David and music composed by Burt Bacharach. First recorded and made popular by Jackie DeShannon and released on April 15, 1965, on the Imperial label.

43. "Aretha Franklin's Eulogy."

44. "Aretha Franklin's Eulogy."

45. "Aretha Franklin's Eulogy."

46. Lucie Edie Campbell, "He'll Understand and Say Well Done," https://hymnary.org/text/if _when_you_give_the_best_of_your_servic.

black church crowd, as Tariq Nasheed says: "All that cowardly 'you's gots to do better' talk ain't fooling these kids."[47] Others labelled the eulogy "a disaster" and questioned how he became the eulogist in the first place. Several said his remarks were not appropriate as a eulogy in a funeral service, though the issues were worthy of further discussion. Understanding the complexities of the eulogy, not mentioning anyone by name, and not sure of the family's wishes, the day after the eulogy, Teresa Fry Brown, the Bandy Professor of Preaching at Emory University's Candler School of Theology, said:

[handwritten margin note: forward writer]

[handwritten margin note: what eulogies are and are not]

> Eulogies are not political fodder...are not "let me get this off my chest" speeches...are not "let me see what dirt I can share on the family or the deceased"...are not personal soapboxes...are not star events...are not throw rocks or eviscerating folk proclamations masquerading as deep prophetic pronouncements...are not let me show you how divisive I can be gender preachments. Eulogies comfort the living, celebrate the dead, help us face our own mortality and usher us to a place of hearing God say, "Well done good and faithful servant."[48]

My goal herein is not to debate responses to the eulogy, but to illustrate the process of what happens when different moral orders and working gospels collide. Williams preached a dangerous eulogy and upset a major section of the dominance hierarchy of the black community. My interest is to study sermons that generate conflict based in competing moral orders and working gospels to help preachers learn how to gain a hearing from as broad of an audience as possible.

The family of Aretha Franklin labeled Williams's eulogy, "offensive and distasteful."[49] Vaughn Franklin, Aretha Franklin's nephew, said that he spoke on behalf of the family and clarified that Aretha Franklin did

47. Ann Zaniewski, "Aretha Franklin Eulogist Takes Heat for Critical Remarks," *Detroit Free Press,* September 1, 2018, https://www.freep.com/story/news/local/michigan/detroit/2018/08/31/aretha-franklin-eulogist-reverend-jasper-williams/1163498002/.

48. Sheila Poole, "Jasper Williams Jr., Pastor Who Delivered Aretha Franklin's Controversial Eulogy, Speaks Out," *The Atlanta Journal-Constitution,* September 1, 2018, https://www.wsbtv.com/news/local/atlanta/pastor-who-delivered-aretha-franklins-controversial-eulogy-speaks-out/825422515.

49. Brian McCollum, "Aretha Franklin Family Responds to Eulogy: 'Distasteful, Offensive,'" Detroit Free Press, September 3, 2018, https://www.freep.com/story/entertainment/music/aretha-franklin/2018/09/03/aretha-franklin-family-responds-eulogy/1188364002/.

not ask Rev. Jasper Williams Jr. to do the eulogy because "dying is a topic
that she never discussed with anyone."[50] He further clarified that the family asked Williams because he had eulogized "our grandfather (Rev. C. L.
Franklin), my aunt (Erma Franklin and my uncle (Cecil Franklin)."[51] He
also mentioned the names of several other people whom Aretha Franklin
admired who would have been outstanding individuals to do the eulogy.
In closing, he said: "We feel that Rev. Jasper Williams used this platform
to push his negative agenda, which as a family, we do not agree with."[52]

In the black community, the major criticism of the eulogy is based in
the overall disagreement with the overarching blanket and broad claim by
Williams that black people had lost their souls. For brevity, I will list four
specific points of critique and refer you back to my summary of the eulogy
for the exact verbiage from the eulogy that is the source of the criticism.
In the close reading of the eulogy, I intentionally quoted and labeled key
criticisms for ease of later reference for interested readers. The four main
points of contention are:

1. Criticism of the civil rights movement: Critics took umbrage
   with Williams's assertion that integration and the civil rights
   movement tore apart black economies that once relied on
   black-owned small businesses, including grocery stores, hotels, insurance companies, and banks. Williams also said that
   black people did not need better houses from government, big
   businesses, and corporations, implying that black people got
   houses handed to them and did not earn them. He even said
   that "black people want to be given too much sometimes."
   It places black people in the state of dependency, which, of
   course, is a cultural stereotype of black people.

2. Black women and single mothers: When Williams emphatically highlighted that black mothers cannot raise a boy to be a
   black man, some felt it demeaned and diminished many black

---

50. McCollum, "Aretha Franklin Family Responds."
51. McCollum, "Aretha Franklin Family Responds."
52. McCollum, "Aretha Franklin Family Responds."

mothers who have, in fact, raised black boys to be men. Some suggested these comments were based in an outdated black male patriarchy.

3. Black Lives Matter and police violence: Because Williams exclusively lifted black people killing other black people, critics felt Williams minimized and dismissed the Black Lives Matter movement and the struggle against police violence. In the service itself, following Williams's eulogy, Stevie Wonder said, in his musical tribute to Franklin, "Black Lives Matter," which many interpreted as a rebuke of Williams's comments about Black Lives Matter.

4. Discussion and emphasis of Rev. Franklin's parenting skills: Critics suggest that Williams's overall point that Franklin's parenting skills released Aretha's gifts to the world was good, but detailing the deficits of Franklin's parenting skills was not necessary and better discussed in private. Despite the plethora of criticism, there was also an abundance of support and affirmation for the eulogy. Many comments surfaced, such as Franklin "spoke truth to power" and "told it like it is." One supporter suggested: "There's a reason Aretha Franklin ASKED Jasper Williams to do her eulogy. She knew what time it was. She knew her people needed some truth. Most will reject it and continue to embrace chaos. Some will hear, learn, and change course. Time is running out."[53] Supporter Bishop Darryl Winston said: "I'm saddened by the ire, and this intergenerational disconnect where you have these young preachers and educated critical thinkers and how they have no RESPECT. I think the way Jasper approached it as a senior statesman. I don't think his intent was to be malicious yet that's how it has been construed. The irony is his call for unity fell on deaf ears, or did it?"[54]

---

53. Zaniewski, "Aretha Franklin's Eulogist Takes Heat for Controversial Remarks," 3.

54. Maynard Eaton, "Rev. Jasper Williams Jr. Tells Eulogy Critics: 'I WAS JUST TELLING THE TRUTH,'" Noble Sol Art Group, September 4, 2018, https://www.noblesol.net/single-post/2018/09/04/Rev-Jasper-Williams-Jr-Tells-Eulogy-Critics-I-WAS-JUST-TELLING-THE-TRUTH.

I will list three specific points of support for Williams's eulogy:

1. The prophetic word often does not make sense: Williams spoke a prophetic word that challenged the status quo and often does not make sense right away. Williams's prophetic witness called the church to take its rightful place in the black community that people will understand in time.

2. When the Spirit speaks, timing and platform are always right: Addressing the question of whether a eulogy was the right venue for Williams's remarks, several responded that whenever the Spirit speaks, it is always the right time. There is never a wrong time for the Spirit to speak truth to power;

3. Williams was chosen by Aretha Franklin/the Franklin family, and they trusted him to address the issues: Therefore, people have no right to criticize whom a person chooses to do their eulogy. Aretha Franklin/the Franklin family chose and trusted him, and that should be the end of it.

The Press Conference
Following the Eulogy[55]

The most vigorous defense of the eulogy was offered by Williams himself in a second press conference called to "explain the Biblical perspective" that formed the basis of the eulogy.[56] While Williams was very conciliatory and open to further dialogue, he was also clear he would not back down, retract, or apologize. Williams was flanked by Rev. Gerald Durley, iconic civil rights leader and prominent leader in the Atlanta religious community, and former Atlanta Chief of Police Eldrin Bell. He opened with an introductory statement and then invited media to ask questions.

---

55. "Pastor Jasper Williams Stands by Aretha Franklin Eulogy Remarks - Full video," YouTube video, https://www.youtube.com/watch?v=UpA6SaLyUWI. September 5, 2018.

56. H. Michael Harvey, "Crusty Jasper Williams Fires Back at Critics," *Medium,* September 2, 2018, 1, https://medium.com/@hmichaelharvey/crusty-jasper-williams-fires-back-at-critics-75763c757593.

Williams addressed whether the eulogy was the appropriate venue to make controversial remarks: "I was the eulogist, no one but me was asked to bring the eulogy. I feel it was appropriate for me to say what I wanted to say and how it is that I wanted to say it."[57] Williams told the Associated Press that he felt his remarks were appropriate "especially after other speakers spoke on the civil rights movement and President Donald Trump."[58] Williams commented that the eulogy honored Aretha Franklin: "I feel I did it appropriately. I think I honored Aretha through it and I feel in honoring her, I picked out various conditions going on in our community."[59] Williams observed that all preachers sometimes do not preach as well as they would like, in fact all preachers "mess up sometimes." There was a specific hardship in doing this eulogy: "After sitting there for seven hours, all the preaching I had in me was gone and I took the opportunity to do the best that I could under the circumstances and situation that I was in. I meant nobody no harm and yet I meant truth."[60]

Williams was asked if he was disturbed by the harshness of critics in the media. He said that he understood the hurt and the pain in the black community and that he would listen to critics and was not going to respond to "you sweet people negatively.... I'll help you, you help us and together we will turn our race around."[61] Williams presented the eulogy as part of a strategy to change America: "In order to change America, we must change black America's culture. We must do it through parenting. In order for parenting to go forth, it has to done in the home."[62] Far from trying to demean Black Lives Matter, black women, or anyone else, Williams commented:

57. Harvey, "Crusty Jasper Williams Fires Back at Critics" 2. .

58. Jonathan Landrum Jr., "Aretha Franklin Funeral Eulogy Slammed; Pastor Stands Firm," *AP News,* September 2, 2018, https://www.yahoo.com/entertainment/pastor-stands-firm-aretha-franklins-funeral-criticism-165138203.html.

59. Harvey, "Crusty Jasper Williams Fires Back at Critics" 4.

60. Harvey, "Crusty Jasper Williams Fires Back at Critics" 4.

61. Harvey, "Crusty Jasper Williams Fires Back at Critics" 4.

62. Landrum, "Aretha Franklin Funeral Eulogy Slammed," 3.

I was trying to show that the movement now is moving and should move in a different direction. . . . What we need to do is create respect among ourselves. Aretha is the person with that song "R-E-S-P-E-C-T" that is laid out for us and what we need to be as a race within ourselves. We need to show each other that. We need to show each other respect. That was the reason why I did it [the eulogy].[63]

Williams said, concerning the pushback, that people misunderstood what he was saying and lamented: "I just wish that someone would understand my heart and understand what I am trying to do instead of making mockery or creating difficulty or spins opposite of what I am intending. That's what hurts me more than anything else."[64] In a bid to include critics in the movement to turn America around, Williams commented:

We ought to respect each other enough to listen. I don't care what another person's opinion is. My opinion alone is not all gold. I am willing to listen to those kids. They've got somethings about themselves we all ought to pattern after, so if I am going to stand up here, I'm not standing up here to be the Lone Ranger, like I know everything, like I have been everywhere and done everything, because I have not. It is going to take all of us to turn Black America around, even those who don't want to help.[65]

Finally, when Williams heard the remarks of the Franklin family in regards to the eulogy, he commented: "That's their opinion. I certainly respect their opinion, and I understand it. I just regret they feel that way."[66]

63. Sarah Taylor, "Reverend at Aretha Franklin's Eulogy Stands by Controversial 'Black Lives Do Not Matter' Remarks," *The Blaze*, September 3, 2018, https://www.theblaze.com/news/2018/09/03/reverend-at-aretha-franklins-funeral-stands-by-controversial-black-lives-do-not-matter-remarks.

64. Allyson and Chiu and Antonia Noori Farzan, "'Offensive and Distasteful': Aretha Franklin's Family Blasts 'Black-on-Black Crime" Eulogy," *Washington Post*, September 4, 2018, 2; https://www.washingtonpost.com/news/morning-mix/wp/2018/09/04/offensive-and-distasteful-aretha-franklins-family-blasts-black-on-black-crime-eulogy/?utm_term=.ba4d087be0a8.

65. "Rev. Jasper Williams Undaunted by Criticism from Aretha Franklin's Family over Eulogy," *Atlanta Business Journal*, September 4, 2018, https://atlbusinessjournal.com/rev-jasper-williams-undauanted-by-criticism-from-aretha-franklins-family-over-eulogy/.

66. Eaton, "Rev. Jasper Williams Jr. Tells Eulogy Critics: 'I WAS JUST TELLING THE TRUTH.'"

Bridging Moral Worldviews

Recalling Lakoff's theory in chapter 2 of the embedded and unconscious nature of moral worldviews and the dual "nation as family" metaphors contending with each other in public and religious life, we can surmise that Williams's eulogy is based in Strict Father morality and much of the opposition is, in all likelihood, based in Nurturant Parent morality. Independents or moderates probably would suggest that the timing of the remarks was not appropriate and more discussion is needed. I imagine that John, whom we met in previous chapter as the average adherent of Strict Father morality who attends the average church in America, would wholeheartedly support and agree with Williams's eulogy. John would find the emphasis on the father in the home as the source of discipline and respect appropriate and true. If the father is not in the home, then there is a lack of discipline and respect, and the result is violence and economic depravity in the community. John would love the fact that Williams put the responsibility on the home and not the government, and on black people and not white people. Blaming societal factors is an excuse, and John would undoubtedly agree with Williams's emphasis on the silence of black people when black people kill other black people and the chaos caused by groups such Black Lives Matter protesting police shootings of black people.

John and other adherents of Strict Father morality would find the eulogy soul stirring, and the call to R-E-S-P-E-C-T in the memory of Aretha Franklin exactly what is needed for the black community to move forward. As an example of Strict Father morality support for the eulogy, this comment was made: "What good is a community without the strength and direction of fatherhood. We see the results every day. Black boys and men slaughter each other by the thousands. Not one can bring correction, because the community has no manhood. Men bring strength, correction, and direction."[67] Following Lakoff, the embedded and unconscious

---

67. Michael King and Christie Ethridge, "Pastor Who Eulogized Aretha Franklin to Elaborate on Controversial Remarks at News Conference," WLTX19, September 2, 2018, https://www.wltx.com /article/news/nation-world/pastor-who-eulogized-aretha-franklin-to-elaborate-on-controversial-remarks -at-news-conference/101-590246198.

worldview of Strict Father morality is expressed in conservative religion that makes for conservative politics. John, along with other Strict Father morality adherents, regardless of gender, race, or demographics, would shower emphatic praise on Williams for the eulogy.

Again, based upon Lakoff's theory, Kathy, whom we met in the previous chapter as the average adherent of Nurturant Parent morality who attends the average church in America, would have the opposite response to the eulogy. Kathy would heavily question Williams's obvious lack of respect for single-parent black women who have raised and will raise strong young people to adulthood, male and female. Because she has a son, she would be very concerned about police violence against black people. She would ask: "Why was it not possible to address black people killing black people *and* police violence killing black people?" She would wonder why Williams did not discuss any of the social, political, economic, and religious forces that played a role in the black community "losing their soul," such as slavery, Jim Crow, racism, and mass incarceration, to mention a few. Not that she would advocate government dependency, but Kathy would raise questions about the government's role, or lack thereof, in helping black communities and the ways in which other communities have received all kinds of government help. She would ask Williams if the *entire* black community had lost its soul. Why not talk about the love, nurture, respect, healing, and self-help that is already operative in the black community? Why did he keep saying, "Black MAN, where is your soul?" He uses male pronouns for God, the human race, and black people. Could he not use more inclusive language? While he might mean the whole human race, the non-inclusive language suggests to her a patriarchal worldview. Are women and children included? Williams's eulogy would stand in opposition to Kathy's embedded and unconscious Nurturant Parent morality and therefore was against her progressive religion that flowed into her progressive politics.

Given that this is only one sermon, we can conclude a few things that might head in the direction of Williams's working gospel. First, God is the creator of all things, and only when God adds God's breath to the human body and spirit do human beings became a living soul. Second, God made

Aretha Franklin the Queen of Soul before the world began. This means God purposes and acts in human history to fulfill God's plans and purposes through human beings. Third, God has a design for the home, and that design is a man and a woman, a father and a mother, a husband and a wife, a provider and a nurturer. Anytime human beings stray from God's design for the home, it will mean havoc, not only in the home, but also in the street. Fourth, God in Jesus is the conquering redemptive force in the world ("Ride on King Jesus!") wanting and working for human beings to respect each other. Finally, we, as human beings, have a responsibility to partner with God and give the best of our service to turn the world around, and God will say, "Well done."

Kathy's working gospel, indicative of Nurturant Parent morality, would be equality for women and not limiting them exclusively to the role of the nurturer. She also would believe that God values a nontraditional understanding of the family, other than a male and female in the home. She would lift the value of single parents, including single parents who have chosen to adopt children. God has a much more diverse and inclusive understanding of family than presented in Williams's eulogy. There are important theological differences that are reflective of different working gospels, but much of the criticism is not in this area, but in the area of social policy.

What is most important for the preacher of a dangerous sermon, and in this case eulogy, is to understand that there are dual embedded moral worldviews in every audience, and the question is how to strategize such as to effectively reach as many people as possible. When we preach dangerous sermons with little understanding of an opposing moral order, we often initiate resistance and antagonism that might have been better managed if we understood Strict Father and Nurturant Parent moralities and different working gospels. The preacher who is aware of different moral orders has a certain moral dexterity and the ability to develop a message that educates, inspires, and invites people beyond unintentional divisive rhetoric and polarizations. The preacher has to frame arguments inclusive of the position of people with a different moral worldview. I do not want to build the impossible expectation that the preacher has to reach all in the audience. Some in the audience are hardcore and will never hear anything from an opposing worldview. Generally, though always present, the hardcore are often not the majority, and there are many people who could be reached if arguments were pitched to and inclusive of some sense of their understanding of the world, God, and the Bible.

I believe that dialogue creates the awareness to fashion arguments that speak across worldviews. Many of us have to get in trouble preaching a dangerous sermon from our worldview, and in the blowback and feedback from what we said, particularly from those of another moral worldview and working gospel, we hear other voices and discover the realities of those of a different moral order. Often, this is a very painful process, and in the pain of the process, we discover that moral progress takes nuance.

Nuance can be defined as the awareness of or ability to express delicate shadings of meaning, feeling, or value. Nuanced discussions start with equanimity, patience, deliberation, multiple conversations, and persistent dialogue. In nuanced conversations, we discover, for example, many variations in moral values, theological belief, and social and economic policy. We learn to avoid blanket and broad generalizations expressive of only one moral worldview and one theological position. For example, when the preacher gets up and says, "God has a design for the home, a man and a woman," nuanced discussion has taught that there are many valuable variations of family. Nuanced discussion teaches us that it is possible to hold the belief that the model would be husband and wife while understanding that God values many variations of family such as singles who adopt children. There are ways to include as many people as possible, but the preacher has to have much conversation and dialogue with different moral orders. There have been many times in my life, as both a pastor and a person, when some person took me to lunch, called me on the phone, or wrote me a note that started a dialogue, the result of which is that I grew and became much more inclusive. I did not necessarily compromise my belief, but I learned how to better include people.

This raises the question how could Williams have been more effective. How could Williams have nuanced his arguments to be more inclusive of those of Nurturant Parent morality? One supporter of Williams published a very thoughtful reflection and apologetic entitled "Seven Reasons Why I Approve of the Rev. Jasper Williams Jr.'s Eulogy at Aretha Franklin's Funeral."[68] She specifically goes down seven points of criticism and nuances Williams's response. I will cite two examples. The first is the criticism that Williams diminished Black Lives Matter:

> There are others who believe that Rev. Williams criticized the Black Lives Matter movement. How Sway? He was saying that black lives do matter. And they matter whether we police officers take them or we take them. Yes, police officers shouldn't kill innocent black people but neither should we....We can support the Black Lives Matter movement AND support eradicating unjust murders in which both parties are black.[69]

The writer is saying, from her perspective, what he meant to say and what she interpreted him to say. But this is not what he said. He did not say we can support both because black life matters regardless of who takes it. Because he did not say it, we are not sure this is what he meant, and he is open to criticism. To say, "we can support both," is to include both moral worldviews, and this is an example of nuance and inclusion.

Second, she addressed the comment by Williams that people in black communities walk around like zombies, dependent on mood-enhancing drugs. Then she says this: "Now, there are other communities who are experiencing this as well (Hello opioid epidemic!)"; and she excuses Williams's exclusion of this based upon the fact that "he was directing the message to the [black] audience."[70] She concludes the matter by asking: "Why is that so upsetting?"[71] Again, she clarifies what he means from her perspective and not what he said. If he had said there are other communities that are suffering from a drug epidemic such as opioids, it would have broadened the issue to make it a human issue, and not just the issue of one deficient community. Many in the black community are tired of

68. Jacqueline J. Holness, "Seven Reasons Why I Approve of the Rev. Jasper Williams Jr.'s Eulogy at Aretha Franklin's Funeral," After the Altar Call, http://www.afterthealtarcall.com/2018/09/02/seven-reasons-why-i-approve-of-the-rev-jasper-williams-jr-s-eulogy-at-arethas-franklins-funeral/.

69. Holness, "Seven Reasons Why I Approve of the Rev. Jasper Williams Jr.'s Eulogy."

70. Holness, "Seven Reasons Why I Approve of the Rev. Jasper Williams Jr.'s Eulogy."

71. Holness, "Seven Reasons Why I Approve of the Rev. Jasper Williams Jr.'s Eulogy."

hearing that their communities are deficient, crime-ridden, gang-infested, war zones, drug dependent, and full of welfare. Williams would have been wise to manage this sensitivity by broadening the issue to a human issue that is also prevalent in other communities.

Finally, Williams said that he "understood the pain," and I believe that he does. I am convinced by the many times I have pored over this eulogy that, as he says, his intention was not to harm anyone. We all need and have had so little training, thinking, or reflection about how to reach other moral worldviews that most of our rhetoric reaches those who agree with us alone. We can unintentionally argue to the audience that is already convinced of our position. I hope this close reading helps us to be more inclusive, to minimize resistance, and to preach sermons that challenge, educate, and inspire both moral orders. Williams was right, "Something must be done, done, done!" And not only in the black community, but also across America and the world, we need to work on the language of inclusion so that we can get something done, together. Aretha Franklin was right, all we need is a little R-E-S-P-E-C-T.

I now want to turn to practical suggestions for surviving a dangerous sermon.

Chapter Five

PRACTICAL SUGGESTIONS AND TWO DANGEROUS SERMONS

Christians must help to remove the poison from the climate of contentiousness in politics, bring back greater respect, composure, and dignity to relationships between parties. Respect for one's neighbor, clemency, capacity for self-criticism: these are the traits that a disciple of Christ must have in all things, even in politics.

—Father Raniero Cantalamessa, O.F. M. Cap

To this point, we have explored working gospels, dominance hierarchies, unconscious and embedded Strict Father and Nurturant Parent moralities, and Rev. Jasper Williams Jr.'s eulogy of Aretha Franklin that generated passionate controversy in the black community along with suggestions as to how the eulogy might have minimized resistance. My overarching purpose has been to examine whether or not preachers being aware of their own working gospel and unconscious moral order makes them more cognizant of the moral order and working gospel of others, and therefore better able to bridge worldviews and develop sermons that invite people beyond accidental and unintentional divisive rhetoric and polarizations.

As I survey this vast spiritual and intellectual territory that we have covered, I am left, at the core of my being, with an even greater awareness

95

and trepidation of this sobering truth: dangerous sermons are really dangerous. Dangerous sermons can cost many sleepless nights, contribute to health problems, complicate congregational issues, and add large amounts of stress to the preacher's family because of ostracism, misunderstandings, accusations, ridicule, isolation, antagonism, abandonment, threats, persecution, and occasionally physical violence. Some preachers have experienced not only loss of fellowship, invitations, and significant relationships, but also loss of status, positions, and even employment. I do not minimize the risk of the call to preach dangerous sermons. My prayer is that all of the work done in this book helps the preacher to think critically and carefully about embedded moral worldviews and to shape the message to give it the best chance to be heard, realizing that no matter how one seeks to include, some will refuse to be persuaded and will lash out at the preacher. Even Jesus, if you remember from our discussion of Luke 4 in chapter 2, experienced rejection and threats of murder in response to his sermon at his home church. Preaching dangerous sermons is a difficult choice, and the choice should be made with eyes wide open.

In this final chapter, I will offer practical suggestions on how to survive a dangerous sermon, which I have gathered during the past thirty-eight years as a preacher, thirty-one of those as a pastor, and the last seven as professor of preaching. After my practical insights on how to survive a dangerous sermon, I will offer two dangerous sermons that take seriously the theory and method outlined herein. The sermons are far from perfect, but my hope is to demonstrate in actual sermonic form how a preacher can think more carefully and critically about the heart of an inclusive faith and preach sermons that bring people together by inspiring wonder, mystery, and hope rather than to justify polarities and one's cultural dominance hierarchy.

Before I go to practical suggestions to survive dangerous sermons, I want to make the connection between prophetic rhetoric and the dangerous sermon. In one of my earlier books, *American Dream 2.0: A Christian Way Out of the Great Recession*, I discussed the media-created firestorm around the sermons of Jeremiah A. Wright Jr., based upon his being, at that time, the pastor of then–presidential candidate Barack Obama.[1] In my analysis of the whole debacle, I quoted the work of M. Cathleen Kaveny, who articulates the danger of prophetic rhetoric and explores prophetic discourse in the public square.[2] I correlate her definition of prophetic rhetoric with my definition of the dangerous sermon, and I want to revisit her work because it so fittingly sets the stage for the practical suggestions and the two dangerous sermons.

Prophetic Discourse in the Public Square

The opening words of this chapter by Father Raniero Cantalamessa that Christians must be political leaven to help remove the poison from the climate of contentiousness in politics often seem like idealistic fantasy rather than a possible reality. All through this book, I have been strongly advocating the rhetoric and language of civility, respect, dialogue, and understanding. This language and reality are very difficult to achieve based upon the broad and pluralistic population in America. The US is a melting pot of diverse cultures, backgrounds, worldviews, and beliefs that create extant possibilities for misunderstanding and conflict resulting in ever-present political, economic, and religious cultural wars. Though Americans have a general agreement to values such as freedom, justice, love, peace, and family, as the saying goes, "the devil is in the details." How these values get expressed in concrete commitments to people of different ethnicities, sexual preferences, genders, social locations, and neighborhoods is a matter of much debate and disagreement. The sad truth is that not everyone is included in the full benefits of the American republic and some want to keep it that way. Some consider themselves to be the "real"

---

1. Frank A. Thomas, "Prophetic Transformation: Jeremiah A. Wright, Jr. and the American Dream," in *American Dream 2.0: A Christian Way Out of the Great Recession* (Nashville: Abingdon Press, 2012), 71–90.

2. M. Cathleen Kaveny. "Prophetic Discourse in the Public Square" (The 2008 Santa Clara Lecture, Santa Clara University, Santa Clara, CA, November 11, 2008), 8. Available at: http://works.bepress.com /kaveny/17/. See also, Cathleen Kaveny, *Prophecy without Contempt: Religious Discourse in the Public Square* (Boston: Harvard University Press, 2016).

Americans, and by doing so they seek to limit the access to the freedoms of the republic to their group only.

Based upon the founding of America on Puritanism, the language and theological symbolism of a "City on a Hill" and the "New Jerusalem" shaped the ethos of political and religious governance. God established a covenant with America, and any time America strayed from the covenant, following the manner of the prophets of the Hebrew Bible, Puritan clergy utilized a form of sermon called "jeremiad" to call the people back to God.[3] The Hebrew prophets (Jeremiah, Isaiah, Amos, and so on) made few attempts at being respectful, civil, composed, or dignified in their critique of Israel, Judah, and the nations. The Hebrew prophets raged and thundered about injustices against the poor and idolatrously following after foreign gods. Hebrew prophets did not worry about working theologies or embedded worldviews or necessarily how to gain a hearing from as broad an audience as possible. They were fundamentally uncompromising, and as a result, as Kaveny argues: (1) the only acceptable response is obedience and repentance on the part of the audience; (2) the prophet is uttering God's word and cannot be quibbled with or debated; (3) prophets leave little room for nuanced, careful distinctions in both law and analysis of moral problems; and (4) prophetic indictments usually mark the end of discussion because those who do not accept the prophet's legitimacy react with indignation to the prophet's stinging words.[4]

I equate dangerous sermons with prophetic discourse, and much prophetic discourse is not necessarily interested in being civil. Many contemporary prophets in the public square, in like manner of the Hebrew prophets, are not calm, measured, and polite. Many American political and religious jeremiads are convinced that to build a society of justice and compassion, it is important to dismiss polite rhetorical niceties and courtesy and operate with disruption and interruption of the established order and the ill-mannered determination to shake up things as a method to speak truth to power. These "American Jeremiahs" follow the rhetorical manners and examples of the Hebrew prophets.

---

3. For more detailed information on the jeremiad, see Frank A. Thomas, "The American Jeremiad and the Cultural Myth of America," in *American Dream 2.0*, 3–13.

4. Kaveny, "Prophetic Discourse in the Public Square," 10.

This prophetic language of judgment and correction is utilized by all sides in American discourse, right or left, liberal or conservative, rich or poor, and sacred or secular. For example, those who defended the institution of slavery as well as the Abolitionists who sought to defeat it both utilized prophetic rhetoric. McCarthyism in the 1950s and the anti-war movement in the 1960s both utilized the language of prophetic indictment. Today, both Trump and Trumpists and those opposed to Trump and Trumpism utilize the language of the prophets.

This common use of prophetic indictment reinforces to me that there are true prophets, false prophets, and those far too eager to prophesy. It is in this regard that I quoted these words of T. S. Eliot in chapter 1:

> The number of people in possession of any criteria for discriminating between good and evil is very small.... The number of the half-alive hungry for any form of spiritual experience, or for what offers itself as spiritual experience, high or low, good or bad is considerable. My own generation has not served them well.... Woe to the foolish prophets who have seen nothing.[5]

For Eliot, society demonstrated moral bankruptcy evidenced in a spiritual desperation. Being spiritually desperate, Eliot believed people often follow prophetic rhetoric based upon the lack of any criteria for discriminating between good and evil. I believe Eliot is right, people are hungry for any form of spiritual experience, or for what offers itself as spiritual experience, high or low, good or bad. Eliot then offers this prophetic indictment of prophets: "Woe to the foolish prophets who have seen nothing." My assumption is that Eliot means that false prophets have seen nothing of spiritual experience, and based upon their deceptive proclamations, many are led astray. What Eliot says of his generation is true of my generation. We have been smitten with an overabundance of false prophets who have seen nothing and use prophetic rhetoric in the service of evil outcomes.

Contributing to the lack of discrimination between good and evil, many speakers and pundits use prophetic rhetoric, and they and the audiences to whom they speak are ignorant of its religious, political, and

5. T. S. Eliot, *After Strange Gods: A Primer of Modern Heresy* (London: Faber and Faber Limited, 1934), 61.

historical significance as jeremiad. Many misappropriate the jeremiad—from its original intent to call the nation back to its founding values for purposes of healing and fulfillment of national purpose—as language that is a weapon to win political, moral, and cultural battles and wars through the missiles of demeaning and injurious insults. Many offer incivility and indictment with religious fervor that leave no possibility for reconciliation and advancement of common purpose, but rather they propel short-term wins to get their way and dismiss what is best for the long-term health of the nation.

Kaveny is tremendously helpful when she argues that "all prophetic rhetoric, even prophetic rhetoric rooted in moral truth [dangerous sermon] has the potential to rip the moral fabric of the community to which it is addressed."[6] Kaveny distinguishes two kinds of prophetic indictments found in the prophetic books of the Hebrew scripture. First, "oracle[s] against the nations" are prophetic utterances in which God punished the nations, excluding Israel and Judah, for their sin, and the punishment often took the form of destruction and obliteration. Second, "oracle[s] against Israel and Judah" are different because God chastises God's people frequently in language as harsh as that of oracles against the nations, but God repeatedly forgives. God often uses the nations to punish Israel and Judah, but in the end, God restores the people and the destruction is undone. Oracles against the nations are not designed to heal a political community and cannot be interpreted as constructive, because they announce destruction and offer no hope of repentance and renewal.

Following Kaveny, a dangerous sermon is a strong and perilous medicine for the body politic. When the human body suffers from the ravages of cancer, chemotherapy can be the hope for restoring health. At the same time, chemotherapy can have destructive consequences and, if not administered properly, can do more harm than good and kill the patient. Kaveny says:

> So too with prophetic indictments [dangerous sermons], which I believe function as a type of *moral* chemotherapy. They can be absolutely necessary to preserve the fundamental moral fabric of the community. At the same

6. Kaveny, "Prophetic Discourse in the Public Square," 3.

time, they can rip a community apart, setting mother against son, sister against brother. This destructive potential is intimately connected with the inner logic of prophetic indictments; it arises from the way in which prophetic interventions affect the ongoing conversation.[7]

In order to mitigate and direct moral chemotherapy to positive healing, Kaveny suggests a helpful "rhetorical stance" for would-be prophets to take toward the community that they are addressing: (1) framing their remarks as oracles against Israel and Judah rather than as oracles against the nations, (2) standing with their audience in the trials and tribulations despite their sin, and (3) calling to repentance are constructive chastisements within horizons of hope and possibilities of community renewal.

With this brief synopsis of Kaveny's insightful thinking on prophetic discourse in the public square, I want to offer practical suggestions and insights on preaching a dangerous sermon.

Practical Suggestions on Preaching Dangerous Sermons

I would like to suggest a few lessons that I have learned attempting to preach dangerous sermons. Many of these suggestions are the result of dialogue in many diverse settings after lectures, teachings, and presentations on how to preach dangerous sermons, and I am deeply indebted to audiences, colleagues, mentors, preachers, students, teachers, and conversation partners who helped me to marshal my experience and clarify my thinking. I am deeply appreciative of the fact that clarity often comes in dialogue.

Every Sermon Cannot Be Dangerous

It is not possible, and definitely not advised, to make every sermon a dangerous sermon when one is the pastor of a congregation. Homiletics professor Kenyatta Gilbert helps preachers everywhere when he highlights

---

7. Kaveny, "Prophetic Discourse in the Public Square," 10.

the "trivocal nature" of black preaching in his book, *The Journey and Promise of African American Preaching*. The preacher, in the totality of the preaching ministry, is prophet, priest, and sage. Some Sundays, as sage, we offer deep and profound wisdom, the wisdom of scripture combined with the wisdom of human experience. Other Sundays, our sermons serve the priestly and sacramental functions of being God's voice to bind up the brokenhearted and comfort the afflicted. Every now and then, when the forces of evil hold sway, the preacher must adopt the prophetic mantle and afflict the comfortable with a dangerous sermon. If one never preaches a dangerous sermon, or if every sermon is a dangerous sermon, the preaching is living in the land of unhealthy extremes.

I cannot give a target percentage for the number of dangerous sermons one should give, nor can I specify what occasions might demand a dangerous sermon. For me, I preach them when I am deeply outraged in my soul, when something is morally egregious, and when I need to speak against unjust dominance hierarchy. Sometimes I change my preplanned sermon in response to immediate events that demand a moral response and sometimes I do not. Sometimes, the subject is best addressed from the pulpit and sometimes in other forums. I cannot even tell you what subject matters should ignite dangerous sermons, because what is dangerous in one congregation and for one preacher might not be dangerous to another congregation and preacher. I can also tell you that there have been preachers who were preaching something that they did not think was dangerous at all, only to be surprised to find that it stirred up a hornet's nest. Dangerous sermons are contextual (the biblical text in the context of church and culture) and relational (the relationship between preacher and people and preacher and God).

There are many more subjects than I have raised herein that have the potential to be dangerous, such as issues of same-sex relationships and marriage, abortion, immigration, racial bias, domestic violence, police violence, divorce, rape, and molestation, to name a few. Each congregation has issues that they would rather the preacher not speak about, and when a preacher discusses these issues, the sermon is considered dangerous.

Many women preachers tell me that in many settings, by the very nature of them being female and functioning in a place of male authority, their sermons are already dangerous. Before they have said a sermonic word, because of their gender and audacity to preach or lead, they upset the moral order and dominance hierarchy. When one's very presence upsets the dominance hierarchy, never—and I do mean never—apologize for being the preacher. When confronted by such, it is a question of authority. By whose authority do you preach? I would hope that as the preacher is standing in front of the people, she would not be dependent upon human authority to preach.

I have found great authority in the fact that the text makes an exegetical and theological claim on the preacher and the people to whom the text speaks. The claim of the text is my authority. Press the theological claim of the text and leave the rest to God. People and the dominance hierarchy are not the source of my authority. I read a tweet by Renita Weems that sums up authority perfectly. She was invited to preach by Pastor Gary V. Simpson at Concord Baptist Church of Brooklyn, New York, which is the pulpit of the late and incomparable Gardner C. Taylor, agreed upon by many as the "Dean of Black Preaching." After the sermon, on social media, there was discussion as to whether or not Taylor supported women preachers. After having an awesome time and delivering a powerful sermon, Weems wrote that she admired his preaching even though she suspected and found out later that he did not believe in women preachers, and she said this: "I did not need his approval. I was fascinated with his gifts and skills and studied that." Not needing approval opens up space to make the choice to appreciate the gifts of a person who does not agree with you and to learn from someone you might not agree with, or not.

A Dangerous Sermon and an Already Difficult Relationship

It is difficult to place dangerous sermons on top of an already difficult pastoral relationship. If a pastor has a conflicted relationship with a congregation or key leaders of said congregation, and then preaches a dangerous sermon, undoubtedly the sermon will become the focal point of the discontent. In many cases, the sermon is not the issue, but rather than deal with complex relationship issues, the sermon becomes the easiest and most tangible way to express discontent. I have painfully learned that the dangerous sermon is only the presenting issue and not necessarily the real issue. Usually, the real issue is somewhere embedded in the breach of some false or real expectation in the relationship. The wise preacher who would preach dangerous sermons would be astute to ascertain, as best as one can know, whether the relationship between pastor and people is on solid footing. When faced with criticism about the sermon, at least suspect that it might be a red herring. Probe for the real issue.

False Separation between Dangerous Sermons and Pastoral Care

As I said in the introduction, I left seminary thinking that prophetic ministry would be tough and that I would have to be a "bull in a china shop" to make things happen and get prophetic ministry done. After many pitfalls and several painful miscues for all involved, I learned the connection between priestly care of the people and dangerous sermons. I learned that the preacher has to shepherd the people at hospital rooms and grave sites; officiate weddings, baby dedications, and anniversary celebrations; and offer counseling and support in times of tragedy—in other words, in times of joy and sorrow and celebration and grief that occupy the daily lives of congregants and their families. I have discovered that it is through the pastoral care ministry that one earns the right to preach dangerous sermons. The preacher cannot come into the church and assume the right to preach dangerous sermons. The preacher has to gain the trust of the people such that the people can be assured that the dangerous sermon, in Kaveny's words, is not an oracle against the nation, but rather constructive chastisement within horizons of hope and possibilities of community renewal.

I once believed that there was a separation between the pastoral care ministry and the preaching ministry of dangerous sermons. The turning point was for me was after my second year of pastoral ministry in my first congregation. After a rocky prophetic start preaching dangerous sermons, one of my major mentors, Henry H. Mitchell, published a sermon entitled "I Sat Where They Sat." The sermon was based upon Ezekiel 3:10-12, 14-15 (CEB):

> He [God] said to me: Human one, listen closely, and take to heart every word I say to you. Then go to the exiles, to your people's children. Whether they listen or not, speak to them and say: The LORD God proclaims! Then a wind lifted me up, and I heard behind me a great quaking sound from his place. Blessed is the LORD's glory!... Then the wind picked me up and took me away. With the LORD's power pressing down against me I went away, bitter and deeply angry, and I came to the exiles who lived beside the Chebar River at Tel-abib. I stayed there among them for seven desolate days.[8]

Mitchell suggested as the focus of the text that the prophet went and sat among the people for seven desolate days and witnessed and was a part of their devastation. Once the prophet saw, felt, and heard the devastation of the people, then the prophet could speak. From that sermon, I went and metaphorically sat for seven days among the people whom God had given me to pastor, and it changed my understanding and my approach. I was no longer a "bull in a china shop." I was a pastor who loved the people deeply and saw, felt, and heard their desolation, and I ministered to them. As I "sat where they sat," they allowed me to preach dangerous sermons.

A Dangerous Sermon and "Getting Stuff Off Your Chest"

There is a vast difference between a dangerous sermon and venting, which is attacking people from the pulpit and abusing people through the sermon because one has been hurt or angered and needing to get "stuff off your chest." One of the tactics of choice is to preach a "white washed tomb, ye workers of iniquity sermon." In this sermon, the preacher takes one of the "Woe" sayings of Jesus in Matthew 23, such as in verses 27-28 (NIV): "Woe to you, teachers of the law and Pharisees, you hypocrites! You are like whitewashed tombs, which look beautiful on the outside but on the inside are full of the bones of the dead and everything unclean. In the same way, on the outside you appear to people as righteous but on the

---

8. The sermon "To Sit Where They Sit" was the fourth of the Lyman Beecher Lectures at Yale Divinity School in 1974. Transcribed in Henry H. Mitchell, *The Recovery of Preaching* (San Francisco: Harper & Row Publishers, 1977), 1–10.

inside you are full of hypocrisy and wickedness." The preacher will wax long and hard about hypocrisy and hypocrites until it is painfully obvious to all that the preacher is talking about church leaders, people in the congregation, or maybe some politician, leader, or personality. When the preacher is confronted about the fact that the sermon was targeted, the preacher will respond, "I was preaching what was in the text." Such hiding hostility behind the text is abusive and cowardly. Dangerous sermons are not abusive and cowardly.

Preachers need places outside of the pulpit where they can vent frustration, hurt, pain, and anger. It could be many different kinds of support, but one source that was always critically important to me was a preacher friend whom I could call once I had finished writing the dangerous sermon to ask for feedback. That friend would be honest with me and tell me if I was venting, unloading my frustration, and taking my unresolved feelings out on the congregation. One Saturday night my tears flowed as this preacher friend told me that my dangerous sermon was negative. I had been deeply hurt and the wound of the pain came out in the sermon. In the midst of the tears, my friend said: "I will stay on the phone with you and you can say whatever you need to say, for as long as you need to say it, but in the pulpit tomorrow, preach the gospel." This relationship was priceless in my life, and even though the truth hurt, it saved me from even more hurt. A preacher who has to vent in the pulpit can access spiritual directors, counselors, clergy friends, family support, and other support systems to express their feelings. I once exposed my raw pain in the pulpit, and my "enemies" feasted on my brokenness. When I heard the things that they said, the total disregard for my pain, I was even more broken. I learned that getting stuff off of my chest in the pulpit is not a dangerous sermon. Getting things off my chest is a matter of private and personal well-being and not the responsibility and business of the people. The church and people are not responsible for our personal well-being.

The Dangerous Sermon and Intellectual Sloppiness

If the preacher is going to preach a dangerous sermon, the preacher cannot engage in intellectual sloppiness and laziness. One of the characteristics of preaching in the internet age is that people with smart phones and tablets can almost instantly research the preacher's assertions. Dangerous sermons have to be fact based, and preachers have to do their homework with accurate and up-to-date information. Sloppy preparation and the quoting of information that a preacher has not appropriately vetted will land that preacher in all kinds of trouble and indefensible positions. The preacher must assume that based upon the nature of the controversial sermon, the sermon will be closely scrutinized. If the sermon has intellectual sloppiness or laziness, it will be undoubtedly detected and exposed by critics. The preacher must have thought through carefully the issue(s), done the homework, considered various sources of information, and placed the issue in its appropriate context.

The dangerous sermon is not the place for what Henry H. Mitchell called "clever negativity." Sayings such as "God did not make Adam and Steve, but Adam and Eve," an obvious verbal assault on same-gender-loving people, garners laughter and far too often audience support and encouragement. At its heart, clever negativity disdains and demeans people. We can beat up on LGBTQI people, gun owners, the rich, the poor, adulterers, sinners, immigrants, black and brown people, whites, and whomever we choose with clever negativity, but in each and every case, it is intellectual laziness and sloppiness. If one is going to disagree, at least have the respect and decency, to present a reasoned, well-thought-out, and compassionate argument. Name-calling, sloganeering, scapegoating, and clever negativity are evidence of a lack of preparation and intellectual sloppiness and will come back to haunt the preacher each and every time.

My goal in a dangerous sermon is to have an issue so well thought out in a balanced presentation that a person had to think carefully and research broadly and deeply to contest me. But despite all of my best efforts, some sought to counter me with pure emotional and ad hominem arguments. There are always those who will not be persuaded. I can be contested, and as much as I do not like it sometimes, I appreciate fair and constructive criticism. However, some criticism is not fair and constructive and must be disposed of in the garbage can, figuratively and/or literally.

An example of criticism that I immediately put in the literal garbage can is anonymous letters. I simply would not read them. If people do not have the courage to put their name on their thoughts and opinions, I do not waste time reading or responding. I learned this after reading an anonymous letter and spending the entire Sunday morning service scanning the congregation, trying to figure out who wrote it. It was a waste of time and energy. I communicated to my staff not to even give anonymous letters to me. My team stopped reading them as well. I communicated to the congregation that they were not being read and encouraged them to put their name on their thoughts and feelings and they would be responded to. The anonymous letters stopped. The preacher has to read them for them to matter.

Build a Ramp for People First

Far too many times in my ministry, when I preached a dangerous sermon, I was neither lazy nor intellectually sloppy but was still misunderstood. I analyzed what the Bible had to say with careful exegesis, read several theologians to get the pros and the cons of the textual argument, prayed over the matter to discern what God would have me say, and talked over my ideas with clergy friends, trusted mentors, friends, and family to have as broad a perspective as possible. I then went to the pulpit on Sunday morning and in a dangerous sermon announced my position.

After far too many instances of being misunderstood, I learned this: build a ramp for people, first. Let's say one of the members who was listening to my dangerous sermon on Sunday morning was a parent who had three small children. The kids throw him off schedule as he prepares to come to church. He gets the car loaded and notices that one of kids has wasted the drink from breakfast all over his shirt. He has to take him and the others kids out the car, change the shirt, and get them all back in the car. He is now running late and his anxiety is rising. He gets in a hurry because he does not like to be late. He takes the kids to children's church. He enters the sanctuary, sits down on the last pew, breathes deeply, and prepares himself to worship, though late and unnerved. Just as he brings his full presence to worship, one of the ushers comes and tells him that one of the children is a disturbance in children's church. He goes down to get the kid, finds out what happened, and marches her back upstairs to sit in adult church with him. He is sitting there fuming, trying to calm down, and the preacher rises and preaches a dangerous sermon. He could not hear the complexity of the message because he was not prepared for the message. His life had been too cluttered, too filled with child care to explore the height and depth of theological issues. For many people, their lives are filled with complex concerns and they do not have the luxury of theological consideration and reflection. While this is an extreme example, the preacher would have helped him if the preacher had built a ramp.

What if the preacher had taken Wednesday night or a couple of Wednesday nights and explored the issue? Maybe brought in a professor to give the depth of interpretation around critical biblical verses and others to talk about the full dimension of the issues from a social perspective. What if the preacher would have had discussion in small groups? What if the pastor had allowed him a chance to ask questions and dialogue in a safe setting before hearing the sermon on Sunday morning? What if the pastor had communicated with the leaders prior to preaching a dangerous sermon? Just because we have thought about the issue in depth does not mean the people have had the same level of engagement. Several times I made a mess of the situation because I did not give the people time. I did not prepare the people. I gave the dangerous sermon and did not build a ramp.

Some of my conversational preaching friends such as Ronald J. Allen and O. Wesley Allen would have probably suggested that I did not involve the people.[9] They would have said that I operated out of the traditional solo holy-person model, in which the preacher goes up to the mountain, like Moses, to get the word from God, and then returns and to give the word back to the people during the sermon. What if pastor and people went up to the mountain together to hear the word? There is great value

---

9. The "conversational school" of preaching believes that the future of preaching is contained in the dialogue and conversations about preaching among many varied constituencies and perspectives, and not the solo act of one preacher. The main proponents are: Lucy Atkinson Rose, John S. McClure, Joseph M. Webb, Ronald J. Allen, and O. Wesley Allen Jr. See Ronald J. Allen and O. Wesley Allen Jr., *The Sermon without End: A Conversational Approach to Preaching* (Nashville: Abingdon Press, 2015).

in the discussion of the dangerous sermon and conversational preaching, but to limit the scope of our inquiry, I will keep moving.

Preaching as a Guest or Associate Minister

One of the practices I have adopted since exclusively preaching as an itinerant preacher is this: if I am going to preach a dangerous sermon in a place where another pastor has pastoral responsibility, it is necessary to discuss the message with the pastor before I preach. My goal is not to leave a mess that the pastor has to clean up. My experience as a pastor was that it took me nineteen Sundays to clean up a false doctrinal position that a visiting preacher took in the pulpit on one Sunday. I had to do yeomen's work to get the people back to a proper biblical understanding. The preacher took a critical doctrinal stand in the sermon and did not talk to me first.

There have been many instances when I have talked to the pastor and sought input before preaching the dangerous sermon. Sometimes I have modified terms, phrases, and sometimes have left something on the cutting floor rather than put the pastor in the untenable position of defending my invitation to preach. In one case, I showed the pastor what I planned to say and the pastor approved. I asked him if he was sure, because I knew that this was going to upset the dominance hierarchy. He took a closer look, and we discussed it in detail, and I preached the sermon. Of course, this is appropriate if one is a guest minister, associate minister, or preaching in any setting where another person is responsible. The very last thing that I want is to preach a dangerous sermon, move on, and the pastor is stuck with having to clean up distress that my words have caused. When I am invited to preach, I come to help the pastor and the church and not add to the pastor's burden. Being invited to preach is a sacred trust and I never want to abuse the privilege.

Be Prepared for Resistance

No matter how well you craft the sermon, how inclusive you attempt to be, and how you cultivate relationships to minimize resistance, you will not be able to do away with resistance. There are always those who refuse to be persuaded, and their resistance can be quite vicious and intense. Some will come up to you and say, "No good minister would preach a sermon like that." As we said earlier, they will go further and lash out, create chaos, threaten, punish, withhold money, stir up a group to oppose the preacher, seek to have the preacher fired, and many other immature and nefarious exercises. One must be prepared for this. It goes with dangerous sermons. I struggled mightily to not take resistance personally.

Taking things personally took me down the rabbit hole of fear, anxiety, situational depression, and many negative emotions. I would tell myself this to avoid the rabbit hole: people play their home movies on my clergy collar. People have in their mind images, pictures, and movies, sometimes of their first pastor, or some other pastor or preacher whom they have had experience with, positively or negatively. Metaphorically, when they look at me, they do not see me; they play homes movies on my clergy collar. Sometimes, it really is not about me, though I function as the presenting issue. Staying with the movie metaphor, my friend, D. Darrell Griffin, argues the church has a movie and, unbeknownst to the preacher, a script and a part for the preacher to play. The preacher enters the congregation in the middle of the movie and when he or she does not play the assigned part, then there is trouble for the preacher.[10]

This is very hard, but I tried to learn not to be fearful of feedback. Rather than being fearful and taking feedback personally, engaging feedback is always better. If someone writes a letter castigating you and your sermon, and signs it, the fact that they have written is an opportunity and an invitation to dialogue. People criticizing you publicly or privately is an opportunity to sit and talk with them. The goal is not to change anyone's mind or to have anyone to change your mind; the goal is dialogue and discussion, such that we can have viewpoints respected rather than demonized and polarized. The people who do not send an email or do not call on the phone or seek to communicate with you are not the ones to be leery of. It is those who work in darkness and secrecy who usually are the

---

10. D. Darrell Griffin, *Navigating Pastoral Leadership in the Transition Zone: Arriving in the Middle of the Movie* (Chicago: MMGI Books, 2012).

most dangerous. I learned to welcome invitations to dialogue. I learned: Have the conversation, be aware, "let it be," and move on. God is the only one who can change hearts.

Get Your Bible and Go to the Sanctuary

In the 1990s, I went to study with Rabbi Edwin Friedman of family systems theory fame.[11] Friedman held seminars in Bethesda, Maryland, for clergy who wanted to learn family systems theory and apply it to the church family. In the mornings, Friedman would teach and discuss theory. In the afternoons, he would seek volunteers to present a congregational situation church that the theory could be applied to for teaching purposes. I remember one afternoon a clergyperson presented a very difficult situation. After an extended discussion time, after the situation had been analyzed from every angle, Friedman said this: "Get your Bible and go to the sanctuary." I was not satisfied with that response. I was there to learn systems theory and I knew about the Bible and the sanctuary before I went. It worried me that day and all the way home. I called Friedman, gingerly expressed my frustration with his response, and asked him exactly what did he mean. He said that sometimes after all the theory has been said and done, one has to get one's Bible and go the sanctuary and sit and talk with the One who called you. He told me that at some point, it goes back to the call. The One who called you will keep the preacher. Even after all these pages of theory and application herein, my reflection at the end is that I needed to have said a whole lot more about prayer, the movement of the Holy Spirit, the call, and the voice of God in preaching dangerous sermons. I found that time after time after time, I had to get my Bible and go to the sanctuary and talk with God. It has been my most valuable resource.

To close this chapter, I present two sermons that illustrate the methods that I have set forth in this book.

---

11. Edwin Friedman, *Generation to Generation: Family Process in Synagogue and Church* (New York: The Guilford Press, 2011).

Two Dangerous Sermons

I thought that it would be helpful to present two dangerous sermons. I believe you will find many of the principles of an inclusive faith tradition that I have discussed in these many pages. The first sermon is entitled "Closing the Great Chasm," and the scriptural text is Luke 16:19-31, the very familiar story of the Rich Man and poor Lazarus. The second sermon is entitled "Get Home Safe," and the scriptural text is Genesis 4:11-16, the story of God's treatment of Cain after he murdered his brother Abel. Abel did not get home safe. I will add reflection questions at the end to facilitate the reader's analysis and applications from the sermon to aid and assist the reader in finding their best inclusive voice for the sermon.

"Closing the Great Chasm" (Luke 16:19-31 NIV)

"But Abraham replied, 'Son, remember that in your lifetime you received your good things, while Lazarus received bad things, but now he is comforted here and you are in agony. And besides all this, between us and you a great chasm has been set in place, so that those who want to go from here to you cannot, nor can anyone cross over from there to us'" (Luke 16:25-26).

Despite the vast and many challenges and issues that we have had and still have in the many years of history as these almost United States, we are again at a place of danger that democracy could perish from the face of the earth. Several times in our history, we have had to confront such challenges, the Civil War, for example being the prime and most difficult occasion, when in the words of Abraham Lincoln, America faced the possibility that "a government of the people, by the people, and for the people would perish from the face of the earth." I know for many of us this sounds alarmist, and full of prophetic hyperbole, but the question that I would ask is this: Do you assume that democracy is some eternal divine mandate and that regardless of our sin, neglect, laziness, and selfishness it can never be lost? It had to be defended in World War II and it has to be defended now. Have we forgotten how fragile democracy is?

Well, scholars charting the health of America's democracy see major threats looming, such as distrust in institutions, attacks on the press, interference from abroad, wealth inequality, and the seemingly ever-deepening division and polarization. It is the polarization, the chasms, the vicious tribalism and division—chasms—that are at the very root of these threats that would rob the nation of any chance for a healthy and inclusive democracy. Some are playing with fire, giving unfettered allegiance and devotion to a party, cable news stations, internet propaganda, conspiracy theories, or a personality rather than the principles of the Constitution and democracy. This makes possible that a government of the people, by the people, and for the people would perish *from* the earth.

Democracy would not perish from an outer enemy, but from an inner enemy. All based upon chasms. Brown people and white people—chasms; urban and rural—chasms; rich and poor—chasm; citizen and immigrant—chasm; Democrat and Republican—chasm; division, polarization—chasms. Chasms, chasms, chasms—all day and every day chasms. I had all of this in me when I read this text in Luke 16:25-26: "But Abraham replied, 'Son, remember that in your lifetime you received your good things, while Lazarus received bad things, but now he is comforted here and you are in agony. And besides all this, between us and you a great chasm has been set in place, so that those who want to go from here to you cannot, nor can anyone cross over from there to us.'" Those in this neighborhood cannot go to that neighborhood over there. Those in this party cannot work with those in that party. Those in this part of the denomination cannot go over there to the other part of the denomination. Those with this sexual preference cannot work with those of another. Chasms!!!

Though the chasm in this text is about rich and poor, I am sure that you could substitute a chasm that is important to you. Maybe the chasm is not outside at all, but maybe the chasm is in your church, denomination, home, or family. We had to hold support sessions for students who, after the last presidential election, were headed home and knew if certain subjects were brought up, chasms would kill family relationships over Thanksgiving and Christmas. I am going to talk about the chasm of the rich and the poor, but feel free to insert any chasm that you would like, for the chasms are legion.

Our text, Luke 16:19-31, describes the rich and sumptuous lifestyle of the Rich Man by stating that he was dressed in both "purple and fine linen," purple, a dyed fabric worn exclusively by the rich, and expensive fine linen that only the wealthy could afford (v. 19). The text suggests the sumptuous and luxurious living accommodations for the Rich Man. Lazarus, by comparison, was a "beggar" and "covered with sores" (v. 20). Lazarus longed to eat even the crumbs that fell from the table of the Rich Man. So desperate was the condition of Lazarus that even the dogs licked his sores (v. 21).

The text inaugurates a stunning reversal: the beggar dies and the angels carry him to Abraham's side (v. 22). Several scholars suggest that Abraham's side might mean that the beggar was reclining at a banquet, like the "feast in the kingdom of God," at which Abraham will be present. It is the fabulous opposite of the poor man's condition on earth. But the Rich Man died, was buried, and found himself in hell. In hell, he experienced "torment." In the midst of his torment, he looked up to heaven and saw "Father Abraham" and probably the extravagant banquet the beggar was enjoying. He was in such agony that he asked that Lazarus be sent to dip the tip of his finger in the water and come and cool his tongue. The Rich Man reiterates, "I am in agony in this fire" (v. 24).

Father Abraham explains that there is a "great chasm" that has been fixed. Those on this side cannot go to the Rich Man's side and the Rich Man cannot come to the side of Father Abraham (vv. 25-26). Father Abraham explains to the Rich Man that in his lifetime he received his "good things," while Lazarus received "bad things." The Rich Man is in torment now and the poor man is comforted. Father Abraham connects the distribution of good and bad things in life with good and bad things in heaven.

The Rich Man asks Father Abraham to send Lazarus to his father's house and let him warn his brothers so that they will not come to the place of torment. Abraham says, "They have Moses and the Prophets; let them listen to them" (v. 29). The Rich Man is not satisfied and by implication suggests that scripture is not enough. The Rich Man says, "If someone from the dead goes to them, will they repent" (v. 30). Father Abraham retorts, "If they do not listen to Moses and the Prophets, they will not be convinced even if someone rises from the dead" (v. 31). This is a beautiful text, full of wonderful insights. I only want to lift up one: I wonder if the message of the text might be that God wants us to close the great chasm.

What strikes me about this text is that even though there is a great chasm between the rich and the poor, we do not actually see either the rich or the poor as full human beings and people. The Rich Man and Lazarus are symbolic of how we see the poor and the afflicted and rich and prosperous among us. We brush by them as full human beings to focus solely on their outward condition and circumstances. Let's look closer at Lazarus first.

Although noted for his physical condition and the lack of material possessions that framed his life, Lazarus is named in the text. We know him by name, and we define him, by his condition; he is desperately poor. In an effort not to be like the Rich Man, we can busy ourselves with mission and charitable acts that make us, at the very least, feel as if we are doing something to make a difference. And to be fair, in all of our kind acts and efforts to serve and to give, we indeed have done something notable. But, at a deeper level, I wonder if we see Lazarus and the poor or do we only see their condition. You can help me, but that does not mean that you see me. You see what I do not have, but do you see what I have?

We do not see that the poor might be rich: poor in material things, but rich in things that really matter, such as family, love, God, and generosity. I certainly do not want to glorify the poor or poverty and whitewash systemic racism, generational poverty, and the complicity of the nation in poverty—that is for another sermon. I do want to note that some of the richest generosity that a person could imagine comes out of the poor. When you see me as a full human being, you see what I do not have and value what I do have.

Huge charity commitments often get headlines. A few years ago, Bill Gates and Warren Buffett convinced forty billionaires to donate at least half of their fortunes. Gates and Buffett unveiled a list and the total promise to that point was $125 billion. While this is impressive, studies show that poor people are actually more charitable than the rich. This was the conclusion of several psychological studies and experiments that clearly demonstrate that the rich are less charitable than the poor. The main variable that consistently explains this pattern of giving and helping and generosity is feelings of sensitivity and care for the welfare of other people and, essentially, the emotion that we call compassion. So it's really compassionate feelings that exist among the poor that are seen to provoke these higher levels of altruism and generosity. What is this about? The research says: "They [the poor] are more dependent on other people to get by, for instance, and previous research has found that, perhaps as a result

117

of that dependency, they display more empathy and are more attuned to other people's body language than the rich. On the flip side, as people attain higher status, their ability to take others' perspectives is diminished."[12] Another study even said this: "Whereas poor individuals may give more of their resources away, rich individuals may tend to preserve and hold onto their wealth. This differential pattern of giving versus saving among rich and poor people could serve to exacerbate economic inequality in society."[13] In some ways, the poor are very rich in life if we would see them and not judge them based upon their material possessions alone. In regards to the poor, we often see what they do not have and do not see what they have.

I also wonder, how many of us recognize the Rich Man. What we notice is his material possessions and lavish earthly life. What we know him for is his possessions, his poor choices, and what he did not do to help Lazarus. He is nameless to us. I often find that wealthy people can also be dismissed based upon their material possessions as much as the poor. We see what they have and do not see what they do not have. They certainly may not need material and financial support but do indeed need our ministry and our connection. Henri Nouwen says, "It is interesting that the term 'personal worth' can mean both the extent of our financial assets and our value as a human being."[14] What about the value of a rich person as a human being? Sometimes they are seen as ATMs. Nouwen said he met many rich people who were rich and also were very poor, poor in other ways. Many are lonely, struggle with being used, with feelings of rejection or de-

---

12. Jason Marsh, "The Poor Give More: A New Study Finds the Rich Are Less Altruistic," *Greater Good Magazine*, August 11, 2010, https://greatergood.berkeley.edu/article/item/the_poor_give_more/.

13. Paul K. Piff, Michael W. Kraus, Stéphane Côté, Bonnie Hayden Cheng, and Dacher Keltner, "Having Less, Giving More: The Influence of Social Class on Prosocial Behavior," *Journal of Personality and Social Psychology 99*, no. 5 (2010): 771–84, http://dx.doi.org/10.1037/a0020092.

14. Henri J. M. Nouwen, *A Spirituality of Fundraising* (Nashville: Upper Room Books, 2010), 29.

pression when the only thing people see them for is their money. In regards to the rich, we see what they have and so do not see what they do not have.

I recall going to see a very wealthy couple about the possibility of donating to our PhD program in African American preaching. We shared together on the mission and vision of the program and our passion to improve preaching. They shared how they had started a business to be able to support ministry to spread the gospel. With great sincerity and love, they talked about the people who had been reached for Christ based on God's favor to the business. They shared their vision and passion. We experienced what we call vision alignment, and it was clear our visions aligned.[15] We do not beg for money; we tell people our vision and hear their vision, and if the Lord provides a common spark, then we enter into relationship. We adopted this from Henri Nouwen: "When we seek to raise fund we are not saying, 'Please, could you help us out because lately, it has been hard.' Rather, we are declaring, 'We have a vision that is amazing and exciting. We are inviting you to invest yourself through the resources that God has given you—your energy, your prayers, and your money—in this work to which God has called us.'"[16]

We thanked the couple for the visit and told them that if they were open, we would like to continue discussion. As we got our things together, they asked the question: "Aren't you going to ask us for any money?" We said, "No! We do not ask anybody for money the first time we meet. Our goal is to check to see if we have vision alignment, and if the visions align, then the money will take care of

15. The "we" of this visit includes the philanthropic strategist of the PhD program in African American preaching and sacred rhetoric at Christian Theological Seminary, Indianapolis, Indiana, Aimee Laramore. Aimee is a philanthropic genius who has taught me a much deeper spirituality of fund-raising and has helped to generate the seed of thought that led to this unique perspective on this text.

16. Nouwen, *Spirituality of Fundraising*, 17.

itself. If the visions do not align, no amount of asking will be beneficial." They had been viewed based upon their material possessions and were asked so regularly that they expected us to ask. They did not realize that we saw them as human beings and that what we wanted was relationship. We saw them as more than their possessions and understood that what we all fundamentally want is relationship. We take money and invest in our vision only if it is good for their spiritual health and journey. Rich people are human beings. We see what they have and what they do not have.

If the poor are human beings and are in the heart of God, would not the rich as human beings be in the heart of God also? Maybe we find it hard to love the rich as we love the poor or love the poor as we love the rich. While we choose sides, the chasm continues to grow. Could we be called in our ministry lives to save Lazarus and the Rich Man, and the communities, neighborhoods, and faith families where the divides between us continue to grow each day. Lazarus and the Rich Man need us, and as we are people of faith, they both need all of us.

While we expect sermons to help the have-nots, and we should preach to them, we also might be called to preach sermons to help the haves. Have we become more comfortable with ministry that focuses on those who seemingly have the least in this world? Are we called to ministry to the rich as well? After all, when the Rich Man in hell asks Father Abraham to go to his five brothers so that they might not go to hell, isn't this a ministry request? Isn't this a call for evangelism? Isn't the rich man declaring that the rich need ministry—prayers, sermons, visits, teachings, and spiritual guidance and direction? I get tired of the preacher who says that the pimp, the prostitute, the drug addict, and the down-and-out need to get saved. What about some of these CFOs and CEOs? What about some of these senators and judges? Some of these presidents and Supreme Court justices? We never talk about them needing to get saved, because we only see what they have and we do not what they do not have.

Might we consider, Lazarus and the Rich Man are simply symbols of those who need us. They are at the extremes of all the people who God has called us into relationship with. Might we live out our Christian witness so that the named and unnamed extremes in our society might be touched, ministered to, healed, and forever changed? Must we wait until the afterlife to rethink what our society could and should look like, who needs help and who shall be redeemed? Maybe as Christians we could promote *a vision of rich people not going to hell and poor people not living in hell on earth*.

With this kind of vision, we are open to ministry that calls us beyond our comfort zone. We speak this vision to extreme views, extreme wealth, extreme poverty, extreme gulfs between us. We declare a commitment to generosity and connectivity. The chasm between us calls for the Christian witness of a different way of life. A way of living that reaches both those with, and those without, to build a community, a society, a world that does not look past any group but looks to heal the gaps that exist among us all. We could promote *a vision today of rich people not going to hell and poor people not living in hell on earth*.

I believe that God is calling you into the gap, to stretch, to build ties with those that you have not communicated with. Is God calling you as an accountability partner, to those who have more than enough, who have not seen a mechanism or vehicle for what to do with their wealth and giving? Is God calling you to disrupt your usual pattern and traditional approach to ministry? Is God calling the poor to go and visit the rich, not for a handout, but for a relationship? Is God calling the rich to go and visit the poor, not to give them something, but for a connection? Is God calling us to minister to the rich and the poor to decrease the great chasm? The opportunity to make a difference will require more than we have ever considered before, a level of generosity, preaching, teaching, connecting, and stewardship, maybe a level of radical hospitality that we have never contemplated. Today, might our compassion for Lazarus and our compassion for the Rich Man call us to Christian connection, Christian community, and Christian witness, which is greater and more generous than we have ever been before.

Why would I ask you for this? Plain and simple, there is only one person who is able to transverse and close the great chasm. Jesus was able to close the gap that was fixed between heaven and hell. Paul says Jesus closed the great chasm. Paul says in 2 Corinthians 8:9 (NIV), "For you know the grace of our Lord Jesus Christ, that though he was rich, yet for your sake he became poor, so that you through his poverty might become rich." There is only one person who is able to transverse and close the great chasm. Do I need to say more? For you Christ closed the great chasm between heaven and earth, between rich and poor, between black and white, between rural and urban, between immigrant and citizen, between you and every chasm. Maybe if we lived a Christian vision of *rich people not going to hell and poor people not living in hell on earth*, democracy would not perish from the face of the earth.

"Get Home Safe"
(Genesis 4:11-16 NIV)

"'Now you are under a curse and driven from the ground, which opened its mouth to receive your brother's blood from your hand. When you work the ground, it will no longer yield its crops for you. You will be a restless wanderer on the earth.' Cain said to the LORD, 'My punishment is more than I can bear. Today you are driving me from the land, and I will be hidden from your presence; I will be a restless wanderer on the earth, and whoever finds me will kill me.' But the LORD said to him, 'Not so; anyone who kills Cain will suffer vengeance seven times over.' Then the LORD put a mark on Cain so that no one who found him would kill him. So Cain went out from the LORD's presence and lived in the land of Nod, east of Eden" (Genesis 4:11-16).

The murder of Laquan McDonald took place on October 20, 2014, in Chicago, Illinois, when the seventeen-year-old African American male was fatally shot sixteen times by Chicago Police Officer Jason Van Dyke. McDonald was reported to have been behaving erratically while walking down the street and holding a knife with a three-inch blade. Initially, internal police reports described the incident similarly and ruled the shooting justified, and Van Dyke was not charged. When the courts forced the police department to release dash cam video of the shooting thirteen months later, it showed McDonald had been walking away from the police officer when he was shot. That same day Officer Van Dyke was charged with first-degree murder and was eventually released on bail. The city of Chicago had already reached a financial settlement with McDonald's family.

Fast forward to October 5, 2018, when Van Dyke was found guilty by a jury of second-degree murder, as well as sixteen counts of aggravated battery with a firearm. Van Dyke's defense team asked the judge to sentence Van Dyke to probation on the second-degree murder conviction alone, while prosecutors argued he should be sentenced on second-degree murder and all sixteen counts. The maximum for those convictions could be as high as ninety-six years, but prosecutors asked a judge for eighteen to twenty years.

On the day that the judge pronounced the sentence, Van Dyke, forty years old, arrived at the courthouse and addressed the court, saying that he prays daily for the soul of Laquan McDonald and that the teen's family was suffering due to his actions. He said he opened fire because he feared for his life and killing McDonald was the last thing he ever wanted to do. He remarked that he was a God-fearing man and a father, and he would live with it for the rest of his life.

There were family members and friends of Laquan McDonald and Jason Van Dyke who addressed the judge before sentencing. Edward Nance and several others testified to the abuse that they had suffered at the hands of Officer Van Dyke. Citizen complaints against Van Dyke were not allowed to be entered in the trial. Prosecutors called four witnesses, all African American men, who testified that Van Dyke was an abusive and an out-of-control officer and was protected by incompetent police oversight agencies. He was accused of using racial slurs. Nance wept uncontrollably as he testified that Van Dyke pulled him out of a car after a 2007 traffic stop, handcuffed him, slammed him against the vehicle twice, and threw him on the floor in the back of a cruiser, injuring him so severely, he later required rotator cuff surgeries on both his shoulders. Several other people confirmed such abusive behavior by Van Dyke to the judge.

Jason Van Dyke's wife, Tiffany Van Dyke, testified her life had been a nightmare. She called her husband a "kind, gentle man" and described him as her "everything," her "other half," and her "heart," "a great human being, a great father, and a wonderful husband."[17] She echoed other family members who testified that her husband isn't racist or full of hatred. She said her two daughters don't eat or sleep and get bullied at school by kids who label their father a murderer. She said her family fields threats and fears for their safety. She began to sob and in deep anguish said: "My biggest fear is that somebody would kill my husband for something he did as a police officer, something he was trained to do. There was no malice, no hatred on that night. He was simply doing his job."[18] When asked what she would say to the McDonald family, she said her family prays for them, and she called McDonald's death a "tragedy." She wanted both sides to have peace. She begged the judge for a lenient sentence, saying her husband would never work again and had already paid the ultimate price. Such is the complexity of our text when it says: And Cain killed his brother Abel.

The first verse of the fourth chapter of Genesis says that Adam lay with his wife Eve, and she gave birth to Cain. Later, they lay again, and Eve brought forth Abel. Cain was a farmer and Abel was a shepherd. They both presented offerings to God. Cain brought forth some of the fruits of the soil; Abel brought fat portions from the firstborn of his flock. God looked with favor on the offerings of Abel and not with favor on the offerings of Cain. The Bible says, "Cain was very angry, and his face was downcast" (v. 5). The Lord said to Cain: "Why are you angry? Why is your face downcast? If you did what is right,

---

17. Megan Crepau, Christy Gutowski, Jason Meisner, and Stacy St. Clair, "Jason Van Dyke Given Relatively Lenient Sentence of under 7 Years in Prison for Laquan McDonald Shooting," *Chicago Tribune*, January 18, 2019, https://www.chicagotribune.com/news/breaking/ct-met-jason-van-dyke-laquan-mcdonald-sentenced-20190118-story.html.

18. Crepau, Gutowski, Meisner, and St. Clair, "Jason Van Dyke Given Relatively Lenient Sentence."

will you not be accepted? But if you do not do what is right, sin is crouching at your door; it desires to have you, but you must rule over it" (v. 6). God is clear that God's lack of favor for Cain's offering was Cain's responsibility and not God's or Abel's. And if Cain was not careful, then sin would master him because it was crouching at his door.

One day, Cain invited his brother to a field, and the Bible says Cain attacked and killed his brother (v. 8). Abel did not get home safe. Right after the fall into sin in the garden in Genesis, we have the first murder, and we have been murdering each other ever since. After the murder, God says to Cain, "Where is your brother Abel?" Cain says, "I don't know. Am I my brother's keeper?" (v. 9). And God says, "What have you done?" (v. 10). What is this evil? What is this senseless and ridiculous act that thou hast committed? What is this abomination? What is this crime? Did you think that I would not see? Did you think that you could hide? Did you think that it would be the end of it with Abel lying in a pool of blood on the ground? And then God speaks one of the most profound statements in scripture: "Listen! Your brother's blood cries out to me from the ground" (v. 10).

In response to the cries of the blood, God says Cain: "Now you are under a curse and driven from the ground, which opened its mouth to receive your brother's blood from your hand. When you work the ground, it will no longer yield its crops for you. You will be a restless wanderer on the earth" (vv. 11-12). First, God places Cain under a curse and the curse means that the ground that opened its mouth to receive Abel's blood is so reviled and repulsed that it will not cooperate with Cain. The ground had been yielding of its fruit to Cain without labor, but because of what he has done, he will now have to labor for crops. Second, Cain will be a restless wanderer on the earth. Cain will not have a home. He has taken a home away from his brother and neither would he have a place. Cain would be a wanderer over the face of the earth.

In response to the curse from God, Cain pleads with God for leniency (vv. 13-14). Cain says to God that he cannot bear his punishment. If he is driven from the land, hidden from God's presence, as a wanderer, whoever finds him will kill him. Cain fears people will treat him just as he treated his brother. God hears his cry for leniency and says: "Not so; anyone who kills Cain will suffer vengeance seven times over" (v. 15). Then the Lord put a mark on Cain so that no one who found him would kill him. God will stop the hand because somebody was going to kill Cain to avenge Abel and somebody was going to kill the one who killed Cain to avenge and the cycle of violence would continue. God desires for the killing and the violence to stop. Cain then leaves the Lord's presence and lived in the land of Nod, east of Eden. The word *Nod* means "wandering." Cain lived in wandering somewhere east of Eden (v. 16).

In the land of wandering, east of Eden, Cain lay with his wife, and she became pregnant and gave birth to Enoch. Cain built a city, and he named it after his son Enoch (v. 17). Cain was able to find a wife, and then he was blessed with a son. Maybe Cain could learn to be family again. Cain founded a city, networks of people, family relationships, kids and grandkids. Cain seems to have a measure of being restored.

God was lenient, merciful: a murderer was not murdered; one who showed no mercy to his brother was shown mercy; the one who violated the covenant of family received a covenant and a family from God. The one who did not protect his brother was protected. The one who was judge, jury, and executioner of his brother did not receive the full measure of the sentencing that was due.

This is a hard text for all of us because what we want is vengeance. I mean Abel is not able to find a wife and found a city. Cain has his life, but Abel has none. Cain has children and grandchildren, but Abel has none. As a result, we want Cain to suffer. An eye for an eye and a tooth for a tooth. Those who live by the sword die by the sword. We want full punishment, under the full measure of the law. We all want that except, of course, when our son, father, husband, daughter, wife, and mother is Cain. Has anybody in your family ever done something stupid and wrong? This is the grace of Almighty God. Many of us want God to kill Cain, not banish him, except when Cain is our child or Cain is our brother or we ourselves are Cain. We would be doing the same thing that Tiffany Van Dyke and the family is doing, pleading for mercy for the life of our husband and father. This is the grace of Almighty God.

What we do not often pay enough attention to is the families who have to deal with the reality of murder. What did mamma Eve, the mother of Cain and Abel, feel when she found that her son had been murdered? That he did not get home safe. And on top of that, the murderer was his brother. What did she feel when she sat at the funeral? Did she make remarks, or was she just silent? What did daddy Adam feel? Did he collapse when he received the news? When he heard that the two brothers were going out together, he knew they would get home safe. How did he—or did he ever—get over this? He had no idea that fights in the backyard between two boys could one day lead to murder. How could he go on?

Murder is very complex. You have one family—the Van Dykes—in their pain and hurt, pleading for leniency and grace and mercy. You have another family—the McDonalds—who in their pain are seeking justice to the full extent of the law. It is easy to stake out simplistic positions; it is very difficult to look at both sides of this issue. Murder is a very complex and complicated thing. Families are casualties of murder. If your son had been killed, you would be doing what the McDonalds are doing.

And if your husband had pulled the trigger, you would be doing what the Van Dyke family is doing. Sometimes we respond based upon the position that we are put in.

Realizing the complexity of all sides, the judge gave a sentence, and his opening remarks were: "No one is going to be happy with my sentencing." The judge called the case a "tragedy for both sides." The judge agreed with the defense to sentence Van Dyke on the second-degree murder charge alone. The judge was lenient and gave him six years and nine months in prison, to which the McDonald family was outraged and even more deeply grieved. They wept bitterly that a police officer killed their family member and all he got was seven years. They asked, "What is the value of a black life in America?" With credit for good behavior, Van Dyke will likely only serve around three years for firing sixteen bullets into Laquan McDonald. The Van Dyke family and their attorneys were ecstatic and said in a press conference that they were going to see their father and husband in potentially three years. I wish that they would not been so ecstatic. I wish that they would have been quiet and just went home. Murder is a complex thing. I wish they would have gone home and kept their joy to themselves because the family of Laquan McDonald will never see their son and brother.

And so what are we left with? Some of us agree with the McDonald family and some of us agree with the Van Dyke family. What are we left with? What I am left with is this: God will take care of Abel. In a time that I do not know when, and in a place that I do not know where, God will make Abel whole. God takes care of Cain; he has the mark of Cain so no one can kill him, and though he is a wanderer, he gets a family and a city. The judge takes care of Van Dyke; he gets leniency and will see his kids and family again, probably in three years. The police family will take financial care of Van Dyke's family. They will get the chance to rebuild their lives. God will take care of Laquan McDonald. Like Abel, he is in God's hands, and God will one day open our eyes to what happens to all victims of murder, something beautiful and wonderful, I believe. The city of Chicago took care of the family of Laquan McDonald with a financial settlement. But, we must ask: Does money replace a child? No! Who will really take care of the family of Laquan McDonald?

In God's name, it is us. We will because we will fight that there not be any more Laquan McDonalds. In the name of God, it is our job to change this system, to elect people who will change this system. It is our job to become judges, district attorneys, and police officers to change this system. Maybe if we could change the system, we could help there be fewer Jason Van Dykes and fewer Laquan McDonalds. The system that we have is not working, and for the sake of Laquan McDonald and Jason Van Dyke and their families, it is up to you and me to change this system.

If we would get together and change things, what would be our goal? The goal would be for everyone to get home safe; that black people and police officers get home safe. You know what the family of Jason Van Dyke wanted that night? For Jason Van Dyke to get home safe. You know what the family of Laquan McDonald wanted that night that? For LaQuan McDonald to get home safe. Maybe we could realize that for every black kid who is unjustifiably shot and killed, it is less safe for police. And for every police officer who is shot and killed, black people are less safe. It is up to you and me, with God's help, to take care of the family of Laquan McDonald by changing this unjust system that helps Cain kill Abel.

Enhancing Your Preaching
of Dangerous Sermons

As I stated in the introduction, one of my major goals in writing this book is to help preachers preach dangerous sermons that assist laypeople and congregations to more carefully discern their moral hierarchy and the moral hierarchy of others—especially those with which they might not agree—in order to overcome division and polarizations that so plague the church, society, and the world. Accomplishing this goal would look like preachers who (1) consciously examine their own moral order and dominance hierarchies, (2) do preparatory work and research to understand opposite and opposing moral hierarchies, (3) do moral and theological reflection to imagine if God was on both sides, (4) practice the rhetorical dexterity required to give the message the best chance to be heard by various audiences, and (5) issue a call to action for change. My hope is that this methodology is reflected in both of the sermons that were offered here.

I would like for the reader to choose one of the two sermons (or maybe both for the really ambitious). Respond to the following five questions on a separate piece of paper after carefully reviewing and reading the sermon(s):

1. What is the preacher's moral order? What is the dominance hierarchy the preacher is attempting to upset? From the sermon itself, can you discern if the preacher is Strict Father or Nurturing Parent morality?

2. Does the sermon demonstrate preparatory work and research to understand and accurately reflect the opposite and opposing moral order and hierarchy?

3. What is the preacher's working gospel? What is the preacher's theological perspective? Does the preacher imagine a God that might be on both sides rather than one or the other? What is common about both sides that presents the opportunity for a mutual understanding of the other?

4. What is the amount of moral and rhetorical dexterity in the sermon? Does the preacher present both sides? What does the preacher do to give the message the best chance to be heard by both audiences?

5. What is the preacher's call to action? What needs to be changed and how does the preacher call for this change?

If the reader considers these five questions as they both prepare and complete their dangerous sermon, my hope is that the sermon will be so well thought-out in a balanced presentation that a listener would have to think carefully and research broadly and deeply to contest the preacher in categories of normal division and polarizations. Though the work of change in the human heart is left to God, I believe that, following these five questions, the preacher can give the inclusive gospel the best chance to be heard.